When the late Eddy Gilmore, the well-known AP correspondent, was stationed in Russia during World War II, he met, and fell in love with, a young Russian girl named Tamara Adamovna Kolb-Chernashova. She, too, soon fell in love with him, even though she thought his name sounded funny and was hard to pronounce.

That was twenty-five years ago, and in the time since then, Tamara and Eddy Gilmore led a thoroughly exciting, if not always comfortable, life together. This book, Tamara's memoirs, tells of the people and places they knew in the past quarter century.

A foreign correspondent's life is often spiced with glamor. With the Gilmores this was the rule rather than the exception. They met most of the crowned heads of Europe, attended their dinner gatherings and danced at their parties; they supped with Mike Todd, clowned with Peter Ustinov, joked with Casey Stengel, and talked about money with J. Paul Getty. And to top it off, Tamara herself has been sent to Siberia by order of Beria, been rescued by John Foster Dulles and Walter Bedell Smith, played jazz with Louis Armstrong, attended theatre with Harry Truman, and socialized with The Maharanee of Cooch Behar.

In the skilled hands of Tamara Gilmore these adventures become a delightful social column about some of the most interesting personalities of Europe and America. Her charming conversational style, her sense of humor, and her wise sense of people and nations make this book a breezy record of twenty-five of the most lively years anyone could enjoy.

Here is an extraordinary story told by an extraordinary woman. It is all absolutely captivating.

Tamara Gilmore and her three children make their home in East Grinstead, England.

ME AND MY AMERICAN HUSBAND

Me and My American Husband

❊❊◈❊▶●◀❊◈❊❊

TAMARA GILMORE

1968

Doubleday & Company, Inc., Garden City, New York

Library of Congress Catalog Card Number 68–10551
Copyright © 1968 by Tamara Gilmore
All Rights Reserved
Printed in the United States of America
First Edition

For
Eddy

ME AND MY AMERICAN HUSBAND

1 "American?" I asked and I am sure my voice was edged with horror. "You mean you are asking me to have a date with a capitalist?"

"He's a capitalist, I suppose," replied my girl friend Tanya, "but he's not a real one. You see, this one's a capitalist without capital."

"You mean some American version of a worker, one of the American proletariat?"

"Oh, he works, or says he does. But come along tonight and see for yourself."

"And who'll you be going with?"

"Another American. Mine's named Dzhon."

This conversation took place in Moscow in the early part of 1942 when the German Army—though beaten back from the very approaches of the city—was still less than ninety miles away.

I was vaguely aware that as the Russians and the Americans were fighting a common enemy in Hitler, they therefore must be allies. I was also abundantly aware that, ally or not, it was nevertheless dangerous to associate with foreigners. Had I not been taught since my first years in a Moscow school that the American capitalist was a natural foe of the Revolution and Communism? Did I not know that in the United States the bosses mercilessly exploited the workers? Had not my teachers reminded me how fortunate I had been to be born in the Soviet Union where a human being was really free and not in the U.S.A. where the situation was otherwise? Why, I could even recite Mayakovsky's "Look and be jealous. I am a citizen of the Soviet Union."

Now I, Tamara Adamovna Kolb-Chernashova, born in Moscow, was being asked to go out on a blind date with an American. Despite a warning light that glimmered—but only very faintly I must admit—in my tiny mind, I went.

Tanya and I met our two American dates on that cold windy corner in front of Moscow's Central Post Office which is about one hundred and fifty yards from the Moscow Art Theatre, and as far as I was concerned that entire evening was so different from anything I had ever known that I might have been taking part in a Chekhov fantasy on the very stage of the Moscow Art Theatre.

First of all, my American date had the strangest name— Eddy Gilmore. For a start this was quite awkward. Why could he not have something normal and easy to pronounce, such as Vladimir Kamenogorsky or Vycheslav Pakhtusov? And then he looked so funny. His face was big, round, and very red and he did not have any too much hair. Also, he was box-shaped, one of the squarest-looking men I had ever seen. He was wrapped in what looked like an extremely warm overcoat, and like the cartoons in *Krokodile* and other Soviet publications of capitalist fascist beasts, the overcoat had a fur collar. Beneath that splendid coat I was certain that Mr. Gilmore had a large round stomach across which must hang a watch chain of pure gold. Yet, there was something about him that I liked. I think it was his manners. He removed his hat when he was introduced. He held my arm when we crossed Gorky Street, at that time of the year caked with ice and slippery.

We met by moonlight and that was the only light, for with Hitler's planes so close to Moscow, a strict blackout was being maintained. The moon was almost full and it seemed to be suspended above the red and white Mossoviet Building at Karl Marx Square as the four of us walked along talking in heaven only knows what language. I spoke a

smattering of French, learned from a French governess which
the family employed before my father's death at the tragically early age of twenty-six, and then I also knew a bit
of German for it was taught in the public schools of Moscow. Gospodin, or "Meester Gilmore," spoke no more Russian than I did English, which was to say hardly any at all.
His German and French were no better than mine either.

"Dzhon," who turned out to be John, knew a number of
Russian nouns and a few verbs so he acted as interpreter.
I am unable to remember if Tanya spoke anything other
than Russian, but she was so pretty she did not have to.

John's difficulty was that he had trouble putting the
right verbs with the proper nouns—and vice versa. For
instance, he would say in Russian, "You will saw food with
us last night?" However, after a lot of arm waving by the
Americans and giggling by Tanya and me, we agreed that
these were very odd persons, and that if all foreigners were
like these two, then foreigners must be a very bizarre lot
indeed. We all seemed to be in agreement, however, that
we were going to dinner together.

Our escorts were strikingly different. Where Meester Gilmore was big, red, plump, and balding, Dzhon, or John,
was short and pale with so much hair that his hands reminded me of my favorite ape at the Moscow zoo. He had
so much hair on the backs of his hands, wrists, and fore-
arms that it stuck out like straw from the sleeves of a scarecrow. I do not want to make John sound like a scarecrow
though, for he was very handsome, with large brown eyes
like a pair of chocolate drops floating in a milk pail.

They escorted us—and that is the word, for they were
so polite compared with young Russian boys my age—up
Gorky Street in the general direction of Yeleseev's marvelous
food store, the one mentioned in Dostoyevsky's *The Brothers
Karamazov*. With the terrible food shortages of the early
war years, Yeleseev's closed, of course, and while our escorts

seemed to be leading us to food, it was the cooked variety we concluded.

Down a dim side street huddling in the moonlight was a long line of silent people queued up before a large door. I glanced at their faces as we neared them. With the collars of their coats turned up against the cold they stood so silently. Suddenly I felt sorry that I had looked at them because they seemed so cold and desperate, in that impassive desperation that is so Russian, a desperation that comes from suffering and the awareness that there is very little that can be done about it.

Our two cavaliers took us to the very head of the queue and John banged smartly on the door. He and Meester Gilmore talked loudly to one another in their strange language while the banging was being done. Finally the door-pounding brought a reaction. On a chain, the door slowly cracked open a bit and I made out—silhouetted against the bright lights within—the head of a middle-aged man with a large black mustache.

"What do you want?" he demanded gruffly.

"Amerikanetz," said John equally as gruff.

The door opened. "Come in, please," said the mustached man. Behind us I heard a chorus of muttering from people in the queue.

"Important foreign guests," snapped the doorman, shutting the heavy door in their faces, locking it, bolting it, and turning on a broad smile as he took our coats. Mine was heavy and padded. I had borrowed it from my sister, Zina, for to tell the truth, I owned no real warm coat in which I could go out in public. My sister was very kind, however, and insisted that I take hers.

John was dressed in a military uniform with brass buttons down the front of his jacket and on each shoulder was what appeared to be a leaf of gold.

"That leaf," I asked Tanya, "is John in some sort of forestry service?"

"Don't be a fool," she said in a loud whisper. "He's a major."

"And what's the other one?"

"A correspondent."

"Why is one a major and the other a correspondent?"

"For the same reason that I'm a musician and you're a dancer, but stop talking and distracting them."

I shut up, but the Americans did not look very distracted whether I talked or said nothing.

John was greeted by a dark fat man who appeared to have something to do with the place, while Meester Gilmore fished a twenty-ruble note from his pocket and handed it to the doorman. It occurred to me that here was a very good way to get a door opened, that is, if you have twenty-ruble notes to spend for this purpose. Yes, Tanya was right, he was a capitalist, and yes, Tanya was wrong. He was not a capitalist without capital. Did he not have such capital that he could give twenty rubles to a doorman?

As the dark, smiling fat man led the four of us down a corridor my knees almost unhinged from what I now know was just about the most delicious smell I have ever smelled. It was the smell of food, succulent, tangy, tantalizing food. The odor was as marvelous as a beautiful dream and like a dream I was momentarily lost in it, carried away with tingling sensations all over my body; a smell that intoxicated as I breathed it, savoring it as a cigarette addict does, as he fills his lungs with the morning's first draw.

In the early days of 1942 the people of Leningrad were starving because the Germans had them all but encircled. While those of us who had not been evacuated from Moscow were not starving, we were often very hungry. My mother, my stepfather, my young brother lived for days on black bread and cabbage soup, and tea, more often than not, unsugared.

On that wintry night twenty-five years ago it became obvious to me that these two Americans, just about the first foreigners, and certainly the first Americans I had ever met, had brought us to a restaurant. It took some time for me to realize it and I should point out that this was the first time I had ever been inside a big, first-class Moscow restaurant. I was also very aware that outside our restaurant my fellow Muscovites were shivering in the cold, taking their chances at being let in, and I was ashamed.

We were led to a large, well-lighted, warm, private dining room overlooking the main restaurant floor. From a little balcony I looked down and straightaway realized the reason for the long queue outside. Every table was taken. Nowhere was there an empty chair.

I was swept up in some sort of euphoria. Perhaps it was the smell of the freshly baked bread and the roasted meat. Whatever it was, I have often tried to remember just how that gorgeous food—caviar, satsivi, shashlik, and more—was set before me. I can only recall that I was so hungry that tears welled up in my eyes. My throat seemed to contract and my mouth felt dry. Never in my life had I seen such a meal as this, and never since the early days of the war had I seen such a huge and beautiful piece of meat. As I remember this I would like to say in all honesty that I had felt guilty at having such a bounty put before me, on a thick linen tablecloth with a freshly starched napkin across my knees, while thousands of my fellow countrymen and countrywomen were cold and hungry and others may have been starving. I repeat, I would like to say that I was guilt-ridden, but I am afraid that I was not. I had been ashamed as I strolled so easily down the heated corridor amid the food smells, but with the food before me, neither shame nor self-reproach were my emotions. Instead, it was fear. A fear that my hunger might embarrass me and give me away and reveal the animal-like something within me that I had never known before. I remember how, for perhaps only a second, a wave of silly doubt swept over me like a balmy wave rolling up some tropical beach. Could this be imitation food like the papier-mâché hams, chops, steaks, and loaves of white bread in the windows of Moscow's almost barren butcher shops, bakeries, and grocery windows? Incidentally, I have always thought that whoever let those life-like peacetime gastronomic window dressings remain in the shop windows along the city's streets, before the envious eyes of hungry people, were extremely insensitive people, to say the least. Anyhow, the horrible thought possessed me for just a flash that the food before me was as unreal as the shops' dummies and that I had become the victim of a cruel and frightening hoax.

Tanya's "What's the matter with you?" snapped me back to a world of reality, and a fairyland of steaming bread, crisp radishes, baby onions, butter, and giant chops of lamb oozing dark brown gravy.

I wanted to stop staring at the food on my plate, but had I looked up my tears would have been too apparent. I said in a shaky voice, "I'm afraid I'm not very hungry."

"Why, you haven't even touched your food," said Tanya.

"I know. I will. I will, though," I stammered.

The two Americans began talking very rapidly to one another. I prayed they were not talking about me, thinking me ungrateful, for this would have been awful.

Meester Gilmore, on whose right I sat, was frowning. It occurred to me then—and often later—that when he was thinking deeply about something he looked like an angry cherub. I later learned that this look did not necessarily mean that he was angry or, for that matter, a cherub. Well, his angry-cherub look vanished suddenly and a big smile seemed to cut his full-moon face in half.

"Za vasha s'drovaya," he said in a most atrocious accent, as he lifted his glass of vodka to me.

I know that I blushed. Never before in my life had anyone made a toast in vodka just to me. I became more flustered and my eyes once more seized on that wonderful food.

"Eat, silly," said my girl friend.

I tried. I buttered a cut of the bread and watched the golden butter melt. I spread on a half spoon of caviar and raised it to my lips. I know that I trembled and I kept saying to myself, "I must never let them know how hungry I am. I must never let them know that this is the first butter I have seen in nearly a year. It would be so shaming if they knew."

I do not know what they must have thought of me, for I tried and tried but I could eat nothing. I suppose I was affected by a combination of teenage shyness, gnawing hunger, the glittering (for me) surroundings, meeting foreigners, and just plain Russianness. Dostoyevsky, I am sure, could have explained it. I cannot.

Throughout the meal I realized that my inability to eat was being commented upon, but mercifully they did not seem to be making any jokes about me, or, if they were, I was unaware of it.

When the evening was over and Tanya and I agreed it was time to go home, Meester Gilmore and John did something that then and there endeared them to me.

As has frequently been my experience with Americans, I could not at first understand what was going on. Americans are so unpredictable. They act and move so quickly, often from a motivation that I neither realize nor understand.

These two Americans began wrapping up all the food in sight.

"God of mine," I exclaimed, "what are they doing?"

"Well, whatever they're doing, they're not stealing it," said Tanya. "It's theirs. I saw them pay for it."

They scooped up my uneaten dinner and every leftover on the table. As the Aragvai, for that is the name of what I still consider the best Georgian restaurant in the world, served tremendous portions, and charged accordingly, there was a small mountain of food unconsumed. Into two parcels our friends loaded the untouched portions of butter, a handful each of radishes and onions, four pieces of shashlik and the white bread, then unobtainable in Moscow's tightly rationed food shops.

Whatever were they up to?

Tanya and I soon found out.

John handed her one of the parcels and Meester Gilmore placed the other in my arms. This was utterly mortifying. They had seen my inability to eat despite my longing to eat. They were taking pity on me. That was it. They were taking pity on me and sending me home like a dumb ravenous animal to devour my dinner alone in my den. How awful. How typical of capitalists.

In the midst of my confusion Meester Gilmore smiled once more and said something that sounded like:

"Furyodawg."

"What?" I asked in Russian, for I did not know what language "Furyodawg" was.

"Fur yo dawg," he said, speaking more slowly.

I still did not understand.

"Woof, woof," he barked.

Was the man crazy?

"He's trying to say the food is for our dogs," said Tanya, who was older and smarter than I.

I started to say I had no dog, and then it came to me that this was the way our Americans were trying to get us to take the load of food home without letting on that they knew it could be put to sound and welcome use at our respective homes.

"What a terribly nice thing to do," I thought, "and what a feast this is going to be for my mother, my sister, my little brother—and *me*."

2   My father was a very young officer in the engineering corps of the Polish Army. During the Russian-Polish troubles of the 1920s he was captured and imprisoned—or put under a sort of house arrest—in the village Garanovo near Ryazan some hundred and twenty-five miles southeast of Moscow. There he met my mother, a slim, dark-haired, dark-eyed girl from a large peasant family. My aunts and uncles have told me that she was the prettiest girl for versts around, which takes in no modest portion of Mother Russia.

As my father became acquainted with his future wife while he was a prisoner in the uniform of the Polish Army, I do not suppose that his detention was in any sense severe. An aunt remembers him as a tall, slender, handsome man, clean-shaven, and though a prisoner of war, one who somehow managed to keep his clothes pressed and extremely clean. At his university he had studied Russian and spoke it well, but with an accent. He also spoke beautiful French, I have been told, for his mother was French.

When the Poles and the new Soviet Government patched up their differences, Captain Adam Kolb was given his complete freedom. In desperate need of engineers, the Russians offered him a post in Moscow and a rather elegant apartment in which to live. To the new bustling capital he brought my mother, then a seventeen-year-old beauty with a strong strain of Tartar blood, and in the apartment on Ulitsa Krasina the newlyweds set up their home. Zina was the first child and I came next. When I was nine months old and my sister just under three, my handsome, pale father became desperately ill from tuberculosis. In those days the wonder drugs for the treatment of a disease so prevalent in Russia did not exist. Tuberculosis was an almost sure killer and I suppose that is why it was called consumption. The best they could do for my poor father was to take him to a sanatorium, feed him with milk in the fresh air and keep him in whatever sun there was. For him and thousands of others, this was no cure and death was not long in coming.

When he was taken ill he was the managing director of a large cigarette manufacturing factory, a factory which he had designed and built. Among the characteristics of the Russian Communists is realism. By that I mean they are practical realists. With my father gone, his young widow and her two girls were shifted into two rooms of what had been my parents' six-room flat. Housing was desperately short in Moscow and two or three families were assigned to what had been our other four rooms, and the bath and kitchen that had been ours became communal. I am not suggesting that my mother was victimized in any way. I am but stating a fact. With my father gone—a man who served well his adopted country—the state owed his widow something, yes, and this was two rooms, not six, communal bath and kitchen, not privacy. Other, more practical work was found for our French governess. It may have been that separated from us she decided to return to her native land. In any case, we never saw her again. My mother, young, strong, but unqualified for any skilled work, was given a job. She became a sort of subforeman on one floor of the factory that my father built and managed. Eventually she was moved up to foreman, a job which she kept until her retirement four years ago.

After about a year my mother remarried, this time to a man a year younger than herself. I remember him well and I am afraid with some bitterness. A son was soon born and my mother and stepfather adored him. Even under the egalitarian state of so-called Socialism, Russia is, I think, a patriarchy. By law woman is man's equal, but in fact I am not quite so sure. Being technically man's equal, there are the exceptional cases of women becoming captains of ships. But by the same standard they share some of the more arduous jobs in the country, such as carrying and laying heavy rails and ties in the construction and repair of railways, and the lifting and bodily transport of bricks and mortar in the building industry. As late as January 1967 the Soviet Government newspaper *Izvestia* was complaining that heavy manual labor was too much for women, saying that it was coarsening them and doing them physical harm.

In Russian families the father's place is the most honored. This is particularly true in villages. With very rare exceptions, the higher echelons of the Communist Party and the Government are peopled by men. Sons somehow seem more honored and cherished than daughters, and as my sister and I were his stepchildren, it was perfectly rational for my new father to show marked preference for his only son. Even at a very young age, I believe, I accepted this as normal. Today, thinking back, I certainly do. It is less easy to rationalize, however, about our second tragedy. When my little brother was six, he and I became desperately ill with scarlet fever. I remember a great deal about this, the hospital, the kind nurses and gentle doctors, and very vividly do I recall a morning when I was sitting up in bed, at last well on the way to recovery. My stepfather entered my room and approached my bed. His young face was haggard and lined and he was crying. This time he brought me no gift, no apple or piece of candy. Instead, he stood over my bed and sobbed. He had just come from my brother's room, but I did not know this. In the midst of his sobbing he looked down at me and said:

"My son, my only son. Why did he have to die while you are alive? Why did it have to be him?"

With that he turned and left me, and this was how I

learned Vovo was dead. It was a great shock to me for, like my stepfather, I too loved Vovo.

I do not think that my stepfather ever forgave me for surviving while his son perished. At the age of eight, what other conclusion could I have come to? Anyhow, from that time on his attitude toward my sister and me was never the same. At times he made us feel guilty for the death of our brother. From his point of view I suppose this was emotionally excusable, but from my sister's and mine, it was not. I am afraid that we became resentful, and this only hardened his attitude toward us. But enough of this. Let me just say that in time another son was born and he too was christened Vladimir and called Vovo.

There was nothing very exceptional about my Moscow childhood. As with thousands of other Russian girls, I dreamed of one day becoming a ballerina, and like a certain percentage of them, I passed the basic tests and at the age of eight years seven months was privileged to be accepted for ballet school. As my home life grew increasingly unhappy, my desire to become a ballerina increased. It obsessed me and I worked dreadfully hard. I soon reached a standard which allowed me to dance an occasional solo. My first one was in the Moscow Hall of Columns, the Noblemen's Club of Tsarist days, and the scene of Stalin's sinister purge trials of the 1930s. It was not long after this that I heard the first talk of war. The English, the French, and the Germans were fighting—although not a lot was being published in our newspapers about it—and I recall hearing older persons saying that they were very much afraid that our country too would become involved.

I am one of the most unpolitical persons anywhere. As a child and young girl I neither understood nor was interested in politics. The same is true today. In Moscow I was completely absorbed in ballet. For one thing, it completely transformed the drabness of postrevolutionary life in a communal apartment—the usual shortages of food, clothes, and other consumer items—into a fairyland of abundances. Ballet was my life. I lived in a dreamland of princesses and princes who spent their lives in gorgeous and colorful costumes, motivated in everything they did by the music of my beloved Tchaikovsky. No, politics was not for me then and it is not for me now. I am baffled by the whole business. How could we, the Soviet people, I kept asking myself, suddenly accept Hitler and his Government, after being taught for years that he was a real and scheming enemy of the USSR, as big an enemy as capitalist America? With the Soviet-Nazi pact the Germans overnight became our friends. In the radio and newspaper accounts of the signing of the pact, Ribbentrop became von Ribbentrop and no longer a sinister villain. I well remember my stepfather muttering:

"I see we've given him a title. Nichevo, in the end it will mean no more to him than the nonaggression agreement will mean to us. War is on the way just as surely as the Volga flows down to the sea."

The day it came was in late June, the place our apartment, and the time shortly before noon. The radio loudspeaker, a sort of electronic keeper of our ideological conscience—and a fixture in every Moscow flat—became silent and then someone who sounded like the voice of doom announced that the German Army, "in crude violation of all agreements and the norms that prevail in civilized nations, had violated the sacred frontiers of the Soviet Fatherland."

War is an ugly word anywhere. In Russia it is a very ugly word, for I know of no nation which bleeds so desperately and profusely in wartime; no large nation which since its inception has been invaded more, whose masses, military and civil, have suffered more cruelly. Throughout Russia's long history the emasculation of the family has become synonymous with war. Those tearful farewells as fathers, husbands, sons, and brothers leave for the wars have, more often than not, been absolute farewells. The Russian soldier fights well, and with his inborn fatalism seldom fights evasively or with caution, almost as if he knows all too well that when a man takes up a rifle it has been written that his chances of returning home whole, or indeed at all, are slim. He makes his peace with himself and then goes into battle. If he exits from the battlefield unscathed, this too has been written. If in some undecipherable roulette of life, Fate chooses him not to die but to emerge unmaimed, well, he is thankful, but he knows it was through no doing of his. What will be will be.

When the great land mass of Russia is convulsed by war the whole country echoes with the sobbing of its women. One hears it along the long length of the Volga at every quay and river station, along the thousands of railway platforms from the Baltic to the Black Sea, from the Pacific to the Sea of Azov and the Caspian; in the millions of villages from White Russia to the tundra of Siberia, wherever the men are assembled to be driven off to the front in trains, trucks, wagons, and sleds. Everywhere, it is always against the mournful obbligato of the heart cries of the womenfolk.

Now on a fine summer morning in 1941 war was with us again, this time as before, with Germany. The loudspeaker was telling us all about it. Turning away from us my mother began to cry. She made no sound but my little brother and I saw the trembling of her shoulders and the lowering of her head. We knew what it meant.

My sister had been out shopping for food. From the expression on her face when she returned I knew that the awesome news had somehow escaped her.

"It's war," I cried out. "The Germans have invaded us."

As the enormity of my announcement sank in, I watched her, transfixed on the corner of a large blue and yellow flower on the carpet. Her large brown eyes widened as if they were elastic and her lips tightened. In her right hand she held the family's weekly supply of eggs. The eggs were in a cone-shaped, open-mouthed parcel of heavy brown paper. As the awfulness of what I told her took possession of her mind, I looked at that funnel of eggs. The open mouth of the package lowered and then the precious eggs, one by one, rolled forward and splattered at her feet.

3 In the early days of the war the German Army blasted and dive-bombed its way through the vast western regions of the Soviet Union, mauling our ill-prepared but amply warned Red Army. In its seemingly unstoppable rush toward Moscow, it captured city after city until, on November 7, 1941, the twenty-fourth anniversary of the Bolshevik Revolution, the Wehrmacht appeared to be on the eve of storming the capital.

Joseph Stalin, under whose cruel police regime I was born and raised, remained in Moscow and on that bleak November afternoon spoke to the people of the USSR. He promised them Hitler could be defeated and said:

"The devil is never as black as he's painted."

Many of us remembered that phrase. Stalin knew Russian well, but as a Georgian he spoke it like a foreigner. His deep gutturals and misplaced accents almost, but not quite, made a mockery of the beautiful Russian language. Yet, in spite of his tortured treatment of my native tongue, I listened spellbound to his speech in that frigid onrushing dusk.

As Churchill's wartime exhortations spurred on the British people, or at least stiffened their morale against the incessant bombings, Stalin's broadcast provoked a tremendous and exciting effect on the inhabitants of Moscow. It was immediate. Dashing out into the street in my warmest clothes I found the sidewalks crowded and people smiling for the first time in weeks and even expressing optimism. Other than this one man's speech, there was not very much to be optimistic about, though, for the German tanks rolled on toward us. Muscovites were being evacuated by the thousands. Those who wanted to leave could leave. We, the members of my family, were offered transport facilities and told we could join any of our numerous relatives in the countryside south of Ryazan, but after talking it over we decided against it. The Bolshoi Ballet, many ministries, and the foreign diplomatic corps were moved out, first to Kazan, the old Tartar city on the middle Volga, and then to Kuibyshev, even more to the south.

December came and with it the coldest weather I had ever known. We little realized it, but if we suffered the German soldiers suffered more. Poorly equipped for a Russian winter, they experienced frostbite by the thousands and their tanks and mobile guns froze in the subzero temperatures. Ever resourceful, they got most of them going again. We talked things over in our icy apartment, questioning our decision to stay on. Our uncertainty was understandable, for hour by hour the war moved closer to us. At night we could now hear the war. To actually hear a war is a shattering experience. It sounded like thunder from a distant storm, but even as a young girl I knew a very powerful war machine was making the sound. Soldiers—how many thousands I did not know—were moving ever on toward my Moscow. At first it was a low sporadic rumbling in the west, but as the days grew shorter and darker the rumbling became louder, until finally gun flashes began lighting up the skies on the old Mozhaisk-Warsaw Road, the road by which Napoleon entered Moscow one hundred and twenty-nine years earlier. The city shuddered from a new evacuation. More factories and government departments were ordered eastward and with them the workers who manned the factories and the offices. The people attached to these enterprises were given no choice. They had to go. The tobacco factory, the one constructed by my father, remained in Moscow. I suppose it was not regarded as a vital enterprise. As a municipal department essential to the daily functioning of Moscow, my stepfather's place of employment also stayed put. So, though we remained in the city throughout the war, it was not solely because we chose to. I remember that one night some government officials came to our flat and after checking our names on a list asked if we wished to be evacuated. As both parents chorused "No," I sighed with relief. I would like to say it was a sigh of patriotic fervor, but it was not.

I loved Moscow. I still do and for a variety of reasons, all of them not as obvious as one might think. No, I did not want to uproot my young life in Russia's largest—one could never call it Russia's gayest or most beautiful—city, but it was both beautiful and gay to a girl of sixteen who knew no other.

I write of course of the early months of the war, before we really began to feel the effects of food rationing; before the fuel gave out; before the pipes that brought heat and water to countless Moscow homes burst; before we commenced burning our furniture in a makeshift brick stove erected on the floor of our living room; before the long lists of casualties began coming in from the front (My step-father's mother lost four sons that first winter and her big house on the outskirts of the capital was destroyed by a German bomb.); before the air raids and the night crying of the frightened children; before the whole nightmare of war was brought home to us, while we huddled in the numbing frost as the rumbling of the war grew louder and the whole western horizon lit up with the flaring of big guns and the bomb and shell bursts; before the Germans all but surrounded Moscow and actually sent patrols across the frozen Moskva River and canal just fourteen miles from where we lived.

Just before the end of the year, however, the Red Army struck back. In the war's worst cold, when the mercury slid down to fifty-two degrees below zero, our ski troops and horsemen cut behind the freezing invaders and slashed their shivering ranks to bits. With their armor stalled, the Germans were hurled back on foot from the capital, never again to threaten it seriously. And we relaxed just a little, attended the occasional dance, and every so often had a date.

4 "Mama," I began, "I met a foreigner tonight. I had dinner with him and look what he has sent us." I unfolded the package from the Aragvai.

"Sent us?" she asked. "What do you mean 'sent us'?"

I explained.

"This was very kind of him. What sort of foreigner is he?"

"An American."

"An American?"

"Oh, Mama, it's all right. The Americans are our allies now."

"Is he nice?"

"I think so. He seemed nice."

"That's what counts," she said. "It doesn't matter whether he's an American or what."

"But you do agree with me that it's all right?"

"Is what all right?"

"You know, going out with a foreigner."

"You forget, my dear. Your father was a foreigner."

"But he wasn't an American."

"What's wrong with Americans?" she asked. "As you say, they're our allies."

"I know, but isn't there something, some law that forbids association with foreigners?"

"If there's a law that forbids our associating with people who are fighting on our side and helping in our war, then it's a pretty poor law."

"Mama, dear Mama, I'm afraid you don't understand."

My stepfather entered the room. "Look what Tamara's

brought us," said my mother. "She has a foreign friend who sent it."

I explained.

"What's the foreigner's nationality?"

"He's an American."

"Thank God," he said with some feeling. "I was afraid you were going to say Japanese."

In those days the Soviet Union had not gone to war with Japan. Our relations, in fact, were highly correct. We had an ambassador in Tokyo. The Japanese had one in Moscow. Large diplomatic missions flourished in both capitals.

I suppose it results from the humiliating defeat of Russia —the world's largest country by one of the world's smallest countries—but the Russian people do not particularly like the Japanese. For that matter they do not care for the Chinese either. Every Russian knows that his country has been invaded from the east far more times than from the west, and far more successfully, too. Tragically, all white races seem to possess degrees of racial prejudice, and the Russians are no exception. I am fully aware that the constitution of the USSR proclaims every man equal regardless of race and that this is constantly repeated by the Communist Party. I feel sure that this official attitude was sincerely arrived at, but I seriously doubt it has ever been sincerely embraced by the people.

"Yes," said my stepfather, "I'm glad this food didn't come from a Japanese."

"You mean that if it had you wouldn't touch it?" asked my mother.

"I didn't say that. I don't pamper my prejudices to that extent."

While I met my first American very early in the year, just after New Year's Day, 1942, several months earlier, through girl friends, I had been introduced to some young men from the British Embassy, a third secretary I think he was, and some sort of officer from the Royal Air Force. John and Nick were terribly nice and we often went to the ballet together, for, as the Germans were pushed back from the city, the ballet and the diplomatic corps returned from Kuibyshev. John lived in a charming little house in the garden of what was the British Consulate. With many other officers, Nick was staying at the headquarters of the British Military Mission.

John and Nick were really my first boy friends, for I never had any serious ones among the Russians. I am not sure why this was, but for one thing, I am not the type that Russian men like. In those early war years I was far too thin for them. Their ideal is shorter and a good deal broader. They like them squat, curvy, and apple-cheeked, not tallish, bony, angular, and with the exaggerated muscles that consistent training for dancing brings about. From my mother, with her strong strain of Tartar blood, I inherited a darker skin than most Russians have. Anyhow, I was not their pin-up type in 1942 any more than I am now.

My association with John and Nick had been an easy one, but Meester Gilmore laid siege to my apartment, and for him this was not as easy as it may seem. With the war my family, along with a great many others, suffered an electronic loss in that the internal security authorities removed our radio set and telephone. We were handed receipts and told they would be returned after victory, but we were given no explanation that I know of. It was whispered about that the Government and the Party did not want to make it too easy for the Soviet people to listen to the propaganda broadcasts by the enemy. Why the telephone was taken out I have not the faintest idea, but for me it made dating difficult. Meester Gilmore, however, found this no great obstacle. He did not depend on the telephone. As a capitalist he had other lines of communication, for he possessed not only an automobile but also a chauffeur. To me, having a chauffeur seemed perfectly normal for an American. Were they not the world's biggest capitalists? When I actually visited the United States I only then realized that while the American may have two and three cars, he seldom employs a chauffeur. But Meester Gilmore was not one of these chauffeurless Americans.

At our first meeting in a weird mixture of German, French, and sign language—at which he was far more articulate than French or German—he asked for my address and telephone number. I wrote down the street and apartment number and I think I convinced him that it was useless trying to telephone me. So, through a prematurely graying man, a driver named Pavel, whose handsome face was crisscrossed in all directions by anxiety lines, Meester Gilmore flooded me with notes in beautiful Russian suggesting that we meet again.

"As he can't speak Russian, how does he write it so well?" I asked Pavel.

"Meester Gilmore is a very gifted man," replied his loyal chauffeur. "He doesn't read music, but he plays the balalaika."

This truly intrigued me—a man who could write what almost amounted to classical Russian, yet could not speak more than a few words of it; one who knew no music, but played the balalaika. Yes, I must see him again.

Throughout the next months I not only saw him again, I saw him again and again and again, usually with his major friend, John, and John's friend Tanya. Meester Gilmore— I think I have always called him that formally—was not like most of the foreigners stationed in Moscow, a balleto- mane. With him it was serious drama and we often went to the Moscow Art Theatre to see Chekhov's *The Cherry Orchard,* and *Uncle Vanya,* and Maxim Gorky's *The Lower Depths.* On one of these occasions he brought along a plump, graying Russian woman with silver-rimmed glasses. She was old enough to be my mother, and perhaps even Meester Gilmore's mother. She was very pleasant and kind and she volunteered that she was his secretary-interpreter. Through her I said that I would like to ask him a personal question, one that had been puzzling me, and this was—

Interrupting me she relayed to him in English what I said.

"He says he's delighted to answer any question. He says that he's delighted that you are interested enough in him to ask questions."

"Then ask him how he is able to write such good Russian in such beautiful handwriting while he seems unable to utter a single Russian word properly?"

She repeated my question to him in English and his large face developed a large smile. He let go a torrent of English and his secretary turned to me and said, "He asks me to inform you that it is I who have been writing those notes—"

"Oh—" I interrupted.

"Don't get the wrong impression," volunteered Madame Tchechova. "I wrote the notes with my pen, but I can assure you they were all his words and thoughts."

This was better. I thought for a moment and then asked another question of the interpreter who, I was quickly learning, was the most literal of persons, one who took everything very, very seriously.

"Do you also play his balalaika for him?"

"What's that? What's that?" She put her earnest face forward, squinting and looking as if she were walking into a strong wind. "What's that about a balalaika?"

"As you write his letters for him I thought that perhaps you also play the balalaika for him."

Madame Tchechova blinked and there was a perplexed frown on her face as she asked:

"Balalaika? Who said anything about a balalaika?"

"I did."

"You did?"

"Yes, I did."

"Why balalaika?" She was now more confused than ever.

From the look on Meester Gilmore's face I could tell that my exchanges in Russian with his secretary were confusing him too. He spoke rapidly to her in English, and when he seemed to have finished, Madame Tchechova turned back to me and said:

"He demands to know why you accuse me of playing the balalaika."

Should I go on with this? She was so terribly serious about the whole business.

"Forget it," I told her. "There's a misunderstanding. I am to blame. I apologize."

"No, no, Tamara Adamovna. It would be very helpful if you could say why you suspect me of playing the balalaika. I have never played this instrument. I do not wish to play it. What could have given you the idea?"

"All right, I'll start all over again."

I was not proud of myself for I had genuinely upset her.

"Pavel, Meester Gilmore's chauffeur, told me that Meester Gilmore wrote Russian but doesn't speak it, that he knows no music yet plays the balalaika. Now"—I paused to emphasize my point for I was getting fed up with this conversation—"as you have just informed me, you write Meester Gilmore's letters to me. I asked you if, this being the case, you also play his balalaika for him? That's all I asked. I was making a joke and I'm very sorry that I did. I apologize to you both. Will you please tell him what I have just said?"

The poor woman. She just stood there frowning and saying nothing.

There are few things more frustrating than listening to a conversation about oneself in a language one does not understand and Meester Gilmore had been listening to a great deal of it. Exploding in English, he and his secretary seemed to be having a very excited argument. At last he inflated his large red cheeks, looking more like an angry

cherub than ever, blew out the air and spoke very slowly
to her. She digested this and said to me:

"He asks if you would like to hear him play the balalaika."

"God of mine," I muttered. "This is what comes of associating with foreigners."

How little did I realize then the facetiousness of what
I was saying.

5 The glacial winter gave way to a warm, beautiful spring and as it did Meester Gilmore and I reached an understanding about our relationship. The decision was brought about by a party—or what happened at a party.

It was one of those big gatherings of foreigners and about twenty or twenty-five Russian girls. In those austere days there were no women in the diplomatic corps and no female secretaries and stenographers at the foreign missions. A war was on, as the saying went, and the various governments sent no families to the war zones so men manned all the clerical posts in the chancelleries. I am sure this suited the Soviet authorities for they had their hands full fighting a war and certainly needed no foreign ladies to add to their troubles.

In a very real sense the relatively few Russian girls who dared to attend the foreign parties had the field to themselves. I do not mean this to sound self-congratulatory in any way, but as there were at least two hundred and fifty American and British males in Moscow, the competition for dates with the few Russian girls was energetic.

The party this particular night was at one of the several houses occupied by the foreign military missions and among those attending was a young British officer with whom I had had several dates. At most of these parties there was a great deal of dancing and no little drinking, the men drinking whisky, gin, and vodka and the girls almost always sticking to Soviet champagne that our hosts seemed to be able to obtain in large quantities. Before this particular evening I do not suppose I had really ever tasted vodka and when it was being consumed about me I did not even like the smell of it. However, this particular young officer kept insisting that I join him in a toast to something silly like "Love and eternal friendship between Great Britain and Russia and to hell with Hitler."

He spoke excellent Russian. Most of the British officers did, while only a few of the Americans mastered our difficult language.

"But I don't drink vodka," I told the young man. He was about twenty-five, with eyes the color of a pair of well-washed blue jeans, a neat black mustache, and square broad shoulders.

"You mean you refuse to drink to British-Russian friendship and Hitler's defeat?"

"Don't be silly, it's not that. I don't drink vodka, but I'll drink champagne."

"No. You're probably too young to understand, but real, sincere toasts can only be drunk in vodka. It's an old Russian custom."

I had never heard of this old Russian custom, but in one's teens there is a great deal that one has never heard of. So, bowing to superior wisdom I shut my eyes and in Russian fashion drained the glass he had been holding out to me. This almost floored me, but I opened my eyes and found I was not only still alive but still standing upright. I also saw Meester Gilmore bearing down on the little knot of officers and girls in which I stood. He did not resemble an angry cherub this time. He looked like a very angry American. During our twenty-five years of marriage, I had only rarely seen that look, but when I saw it, it meant trouble coupled with action.

I did not understand what he said to my English friend or what the officer said to Meester Gilmore, but they were not exchanging compliments. Just the opposite, I would say.

However little of what they were saying I may have understood, I was certain that they were shouting at one another about me. Suddenly my two friends were fighting, but it was all over quite quickly, and to my embarrassment—and most definitely to his—the young officer was knocked to the floor. He got up very smartly but went down again. By now the large room was filled with the noise of shouting and screaming. In the excitement someone got between me and the action, screening my view, but over uniformed shoulders and the heads of Russian females, I saw my young English friend being thrown through the front door into the slush outside by my American friend.

I try to avoid arguments. I despise controversy. I abhor fighting and any form of violence. I hate to confess this, but on that particular evening I felt a tiny glow of pride or something at being the cause of a fist fight between two grown men.

Over the years I have learned that the British have a marvelous sense of humor. Of all the people in the world they seem to laugh more easily at themselves. A short, fat, bald British colonel, whose Russian was perfect, leaned toward me and said into my ear above the din:

"Now, my dear, you can understand why and how the English lost the American revolution."

Talk about Russians being strange, what about Americans and Englishmen? Less than a week after the fight the British officer, who had been pitched into the slushy street, and Meester Gilmore were laughing and joking together as if nothing had ever happened.

Incidentally, on the way home after the party fight—and God only knows how we understood one another but our understanding was unmistakable—Meester Gilmore and I reached an accord. From then on I was his girl.

During the long years when Joseph Stalin dominated over two hundred million Soviet citizens, every Russian girl who kept company with a foreigner came under a sort of double suspicion. The foreigners usually regarded her as an espionage agent, or at least an informer of the secret police, and the Soviet authorities considered her a spy working for foreign powers, or if not that, then a poor security risk. In the majority of cases neither view was correct. What sort of useful information could the poor girls have possessed? My mind boggles at the very supposition.

Now I do not mean to say that there were no Russian girls passing on some sort of information to the espionage and counterespionage authorities in Moscow, but I refuse to think that it could have been of much value. I am certain that some girls cooperated with the shadowy forces that were such a part of everyday life under Stalin, but only one of them ever confided in me. She was one of the girls who, year after year, seemed to get into no trouble because of their association with foreigners temporarily resident in the USSR. I know it for a fact in only one case, but I think one may safely assume that these few girls had special permission, or even directives, to keep company with certain men. I knew one quite pretty girl whose friends were always air force officers, generally American or British. When one finished his Russian tour of duty, she seemed automatically to take up with his successor. I had been introduced to a trim red-haired girl who seldom, if ever, associated with anyone except naval officers. Two or three of these girls lived openly with their admirers, walking innocently or arrogantly past the uniformed militiamen who were stationed outside almost every house or apartment occupied by Americans, Britons, Australians, Frenchmen, New Zealanders, or Canadians. The militiamen neither stopped them, challenged them, nor questioned them, which, I can assure you, was not the case with other Soviet citizens who tried to enter the foreigner's house.

About the one who confided in me:

She came from a family whose name has long been prominent in Russian history, but of course under the tsars. She told me that from time to time the Soviet security organs asked her to find out what her various boy friends thought about this or that subject, what people they saw, and if her foreign friends ever expressed anti-Soviet or even critical opinions of Stalin and his Government.

Weeping quietly as we sat on a park bench where no one could hear us, or where no planted listening device could pick up our conversation, she told me that under threats she reported on the man she loved.

"What did they threaten you with?" I asked.

"They said they would arrest my mother."

I knew that this wretched girl's father had been arrested during the purges of the 1930s and executed. Under the intimidation to involve her mother she cooperated.

"I loathe myself for doing it," she said very quietly.

There has been a great deal of speculation in the United States, England, and elsewhere about the Russian girls who associated with foreigners. To believe some of the accounts, a few of the girls must have been super Mata Haris endowed with the resourcefulness of James Bonds.

In the early days of the war I think that most of the girls who attended foreign parties in Moscow—and I include myself—saw these men from far-off lands because they were interesting, different, and exciting. One must also be frank about something else. In those days of bleak austerity, having a good hot meal in well-heated surroundings was pleasant, and many of us were young and inexperienced in life. We knew we were taking risks, though. We knew for certain, or had heard, that associating with foreigners without permission was forbidden and could be punished by banishment from Moscow or worse. "But whose permission?" I once asked myself. "And where do you apply for it?"

For myself I reasoned that the Americans and British and the others were now our allies, and that while associating with a foreigner in the past may have been forbidden, this was no longer the case. I thought that this surely must apply to the Americans, for they were supplying us with so many vital war materials as well as large amounts of food. Well, this is what I thought.

Then it happened.

It was a brilliant spring day when the cloudless blue sky looked to me like one vast field of hyacinths and robin's eggs; when the birds were playing piccolos to one another; when the buds on the trees and shrubs seemed to swell before your very eyes; when the long, cold, dark winter had been driven to some other part of the world; when the first promise of the white nights of Russia and a warm summer was in the fresh and blissful air, and when I was in love for the very first time. It was then that the fragile roof of my snug little world caved in.

My mother had asked me to go to a peasant market near our house and do what shopping could be done there. I carried a string bag—then a nation-wide shopping device— with me. I walked along singing to myself and joined the crowds in the big open-space market. A crowd of several hundred, mostly women, swarmed about the peasants who had brought various produce to the city to sell at whatever prices they could get, this depending on its availability, or lack of availability, at the state food shops where severe rationing prevailed.

Just to my left someone spoke to me.

"Tamara Adamovna." I turned and saw a uniformed militiaman.

"Yes?"

"Your documents, please."

Every Soviet citizen carries identification papers in the form of an internal passport that bears the owner's full name, date of birth, place of residence, and nationality— in my case, Russian.

"Why do you want my documents? I haven't done anything wrong."

"I must see your documents," he insisted.

"They're at home, but what have I done?"

"You don't have your documents?"

I told you they are at home. I live very close on Ulitsa Krasina."

"You have no documents. You must come with me."

I protested but I saw he meant business. I walked alongside him as we headed toward the less crowded street. He led me to two men in dark suits and peaked cloth caps, the unofficial uniform that most Muscovites recognized as belonging to the secret police of the dreaded L. P. Beria. Now I was truly frightened.

"She has no documents," said the militiaman.

"All right," said one of the plainclothesmen. "Come with us. Here, this way."

"But what have I done?" The weakness of my own voice startled me. There was no reply.

I was put into the rear seat of a black automobile. As the two policemen sat down on either side of me the militiaman climbed in beside the driver. In my growing fear I felt as if I were suffocating.

In those days there were very few cars in Moscow and those that were about belonged to the Government, black and curtained and one very much like the other. As we rode along my captors were silent. Because of the curtains I could see where we were going only by looking through a narrow space between the heads of the driver and the militiaman on the front seat, and I very much wanted to know where we were going. All too soon it became abundantly apparent.

Near the center of the city the car turned into the rear courtyard of the most frightening building in the whole Soviet Union, the Lubyanka, headquarters of the correctly feared secret police, then known as the NKVD.

The enormity of what was happening to me all but made me physically sick. Everyone, I believe—from the Siberian peasant to the Leningrad intellectual—had heard whispered stories of people entering this building who were never seen again. Stories were told and retold of the terrible things that went on inside; of cells where the lights remained on day and night, where there was no privacy from the jailer who observed one's every action through peepholes in the steel doors; horror tales of beatings and executions in the subterranean corridors; how after small rubber balls were placed into the mouths of the accused, the victims were told to stand and face one of the corridor's whitewashed walls, and how standing there with the balls in their mouths, they were shot in the back of their heads at the base of their brains. The rubber balls served a useful but gruesome purpose. They prevented messes on the walls and floors.

These were just some of my thoughts as I was led into the somber old building, put into an elevator, lifted to the fourth or fifth floor, led down a carpeted corridor, and told to sit on one of several wrought-iron chairs beside a wooden door. Like raw photographic film, my frightened eyes recorded everything in sight. The plainclothesmen took their places beside me and after we had been sitting like this— without a word being spoken by anyone—a youngish man in uniform appeared and motioned me to follow him through a big door in the right-hand wall.

Inside the room all the curtains were drawn. It was large and rather expensively furnished and bright lights seemed to be everywhere. There were several leather-covered armchairs and a leather-covered sofa and down at one end a tremendous desk behind which sat an officer in the uniform of the NKVD. The young man who brought me into this office addressed him as "Comrade General."

"My God," I thought, "what crime have I committed that I am brought before a general?"

The general rose and pointed to one of the chairs. As the young officer left me alone with his superior, a rather handsome dark, gray man, I sat down a very terrified girl.

"Tamara Adamovna," he began, "I suppose you know why it's been necessary to bring you here."

"No, I don't," I managed to say.

"You must know," he said, with a frown. "It must be the most apparent thing in life."

"I'm terribly sorry, but I just don't—" I recall raising my hands in an imploring gesture.

This conversation took place a long time ago, but I remember it vividly. His words burned into my brain with such intensity that I am sure they will remain forever etched there.

"You are here because you have been degrading yourself and betraying your country and our wise and fatherly Government by your persistent association with foreigners, and in particular one foreigner."

There was a cold hard edge to his voice.

Thoroughly frightened though I was, this was a bit too much.

"But the Americans are our allies," I managed to say.

"Allies?" he said contemptuously. "Yes, in their own words they see themselves as our allies, but do they open up a second front? No, of course they don't. Like cowardly dogs they hang back, afraid to fight, licking their rotten capitalist lips as our Soviet Motherland is bled of its manhood. In their scandal-mongering newspapers and over their gossipy radios they call us their allies. Oh, yes, we are on the same side against Hitler, but this is only one of those accidents of history. Had not America been dragged into the war to save her English lackeys, the American bosses would have happily stayed where they were, exploiting their masses and stuffing their fat bellies while we remain in a death lock with the fascist beasts."

He stopped and moistened his lips with his tongue. I noticed that he had a gold tooth.

"And you, Tamara Adamovna, who have been so lucky as to be born in the world's most advanced Socialist country, a true democracy of the people, you have forgotten what you owe to your dear Motherland for giving you an education, for giving you a warm clean home. You have forgotten your great personal debt to Comrade Stalin, who always has your welfare at heart."

On and on he went in this fashion and the more he talked the less convincing he seemed. I was still afraid, terribly afraid, but my fear pulverized me no longer. I began to get a better grip on myself, to fight back my hysteria and, how ironic it seems today, but to take comfort in Stalin's wartime assurance that the Devil is never as black as he is painted.

Next the general lectured me about my family. He seemed to know everything—names, dates, places. He reeled off a list of my closest Russian friends before he got to the subject of Eddy Gilmore.

Every so often he would stop and wet his lips, a gesture I began to welcome as a respite, however brief, from his accusations. He told me far more about Eddy than I knew; so many details, in fact, that I began to question them. How was it possible for this man to know the Christian name of Gilmore's mother and where she lived?

"You are being corrupted by an enemy of your country," he said, and as he said that I suddenly remembered how Eddy and another American correspondent, Meyer Handler, answered an appeal for blood donors and had given their blood at a Red Army hospital. Their blood-giving had been filmed by Soviet cameramen and screened in Moscow cinemas.

The longer the general talked the more he seemed to be going over a set speech, and every time he stopped to moisten his lips, it was as if he had just completed a chapter in some document that he had read before, and having done that, was pausing before going on to another.

"I have a daughter your age," he said and his gold tooth sparkled in the room's harsh electric light. "I would prefer to see her dead than to have put herself in your position.

This man, this American, is playing with you. You are his toy."

"He has told me he wants to marry me," I managed to spurt out.

"Marry you?" He laughed a very loud laugh. "He will never marry you. Never."

I remained silent. Perhaps the general was right.

There was a clock in my accuser's office, hanging on the wall between an engraving of Lenin and of Stalin. I faced the clock and from time to time—when the general seemed to rest between his chapters of vilification—I would glance at the clock. Unless I was losing my mind I had been sitting there for almost five hours. Five whole hours in that same chair. Had it not been deep and soft I do not suppose I could have gone through the ordeal.

At last it was over.

"So," he said and his lips snapped shut as if he were closing a book, "for your own good and protection you are being banished to Shadrinsk."

Oh, no! Not that, surely?

"You will be given travel documents, your railway ticket, and you have forty-eight hours in which to leave Moscow. You are in very serious trouble. It's possible you will be in even more serious trouble should you fail to carry out every detail of this order. Do you understand?"

I nodded, for I seriously doubt if I could have spoken. Shadrinsk. I had heard the name all right, as many Soviet citizens have heard it. It was an awesome name. All I could remember hearing about it was that it was somewhere in Siberia and that once having been sent there, people were not in the habit of returning.

Rising from his chair the general called for his adjutant, who almost automatically appeared in the doorway.

"Before you receive your documents," said my accuser, "you must sign this."

The young officer placed a printed sheet of paper before

me and pointed to an inkwell and pen. With his forefinger he indicated a line at the bottom of the page. I signed my name.

"Don't bother about the date," he said in a very soft voice, "we'll fill that in."

"Do you know what you have signed?" asked the general.

"No, I'm not sure."

"You have signed a promise to reveal nothing of this meeting with me, especially to your American." He made "your American" sound like two very unpleasant words.

I did not reply.

His final words were, "Remember, you have forty-eight hours in which to leave Moscow."

Again I said nothing. There was nothing to say. At first I had been terrified. Now I was more stunned than terrified. The next thing that I remember was being taken to another office by the two plainclothesmen who had been waiting. I was handed some papers, and clutching them—for I felt a real need to hold on to something—I was led out of the Lubyanka, across the courtyard, and put into the same curtained automobile.

"We are taking you to your home," said one of the men. He seemed to be a voice in some nightmare.

"No, please," I begged. "Let me walk. Let me off anywhere. Anywhere will do."

I was determined not to let one thing happen. My mother must not be disgraced by having a car of the secret police dump me on her doorstep.

"All right," said the man. In silence we drove until we turned into a side street near the old-fashioned apartment house where we lived. Still clinging to my banishment papers I got out of the car. I clung to them as if they were some new lease on life, whereas, of course, they were just the opposite.

I have been gravely ill in my life. I have given birth to three children. I have once been let down and terribly dis-

appointed by a close friend, and with all the somber moments there has been a lot of gaiety, but looking back on
everything, I believe those moments in that police car,
clutching my passport to Siberia, was the blackest despair
I have ever known.

6 When I entered our apartment I saw the look of relief on my mother's face. Never one to scold, complain, or accuse, she smiled faintly and let out a little sigh.

"You're home," was all she said.

"Yes, I'm home, Mama, but I'm afraid it's not for very long."

I blurted out what had happened.

When I finished she said, "First of all, I think you'd better tell Eddy. He's been worried sick over you."

She kissed me and looked into my face for what seemed a long time and then said, "No, first of all you must go to bed. We'll get word to him that you're safe."

"Safe?" thought I.

My sister went to see Eddy, who lived on Ulitsa Shchukina, about two miles from us, and told him generally what she had learned from me, omitting the Lubyanka details. She made him understand, however, that I would have to leave Moscow very shortly.

"How did he take it?" I asked.

"He was, how shall I put it, crazy with grief."

"Poor Meester Gilmore."

"Poor Tamara," said Zina.

"Are you sure he understood you?"

"His Russian is improving all the time."

As low as I felt I could not resist saying, "Not this one."

Before the night was over his secretary-interpreter arrived at our apartment and I related to her as much of my story as I dared. Rather dramatically I also asked her to tell him that this was probably farewell forever, for I must go to far-off Shadrinsk within twenty-four hours.

When banishment to Siberia is the issue, forty-eight hours is not a very long time in which to get things done with a mammoth bureaucracy, but my mother and Eddy Gilmore made the best of the time they had. They decided that she should appeal to the authorities, not against my being sent away, but against the harshness of banishment to Siberia on a young girl who had spent most of her life as a student in a ballet school. She would say to them that surely a mistake must have been made somewhere; that as Soviet punishment was based on correction, my errant ways could better be corrected in a less harsh atmosphere than a concentration camp in Siberia.

On his own Eddy unfolded the story of our romance to the chief of the Soviet press department, his logical official contact with the Government. A strange, tall, bushy-haired, myopic man, N. G. Palgunov showed unexpected sympathy and emphasized that while he could promise nothing, he would think matters over and see if there were anything that might be done. Eddy's loyal journalist colleagues rallied round and actually sent off an appeal to Stalin and to Beria, the ill-fated and generally despised secret police chieftain.

I have a feeling that somewhere in the vast, oppressive police system there must have been at least one human with a touch of softness in his character. In saying this I am sure that I must be in a minority of one to several million, but I long ago learned that no man is all bad, that there is some good in all of us and some molecule of compassion in the hardest of individuals. When Stalin was sending thousands of people to their deaths during the purges of the 1930s he was, at the very same time, writing touchingly sweet letters to his daughter Svetlana and signing them "Little Papa." In any case, my mother was summoned to a sort of central bureau of documents and told that my case had been reviewed and that while my banishment was just and legal and, under the circumstances necessary, her request had been granted. I did not have to go to Shadrinsk, but as my mother had suggested, I could stay with her relatives in the village about six miles south of Ryazan. We all rejoiced and gave thanks for this change of heart—somewhere.

One feature of the police action against me has always been a mystery. In the general's long and scathing denunciation of me, his criticisms were always along political and ideological lines—that I a Soviet citizen had acted contrary to the norms of behavior laid down by the Communist Party and the Soviet Government. No moral accusation had been made against me. It was political and I, in a sense, had become a political prisoner, punished by banishment from Moscow. A political prisoner at the age of seventeen!

I gathered that as I was being forced to leave Moscow, perhaps forever, there would be no objection to saying good-bye to the man I loved. This turned out to be a very emotional scene and it upsets me today even to think about it.

Meester Gilmore enveloped me in his large arms.

"Never forget," he said very slowly in English, for as he had made progress with the Russian language I had been learning English, "how deeply and tenderly I love you. And never, never forget that I know that I am responsible for your trouble—"

"Oh, no," I protested in Russian. "You are not to blame."

"Ah, but I am. I've brought this terrible misfortune on you and your family."

"No. No. None of us believes that."

Shaking his head as if to dismiss my protest he said, "Please believe in me and have faith in me. God knows how I'll do it, but somehow it's going to be done. I'll get you back to Moscow, and I'll also work it out how we can get married."

"Marry me?" At that time nothing that I could imagine seemed less probable.

"Yes," he said. "I suppose I should have asked your mother and—"

"Honey," I said—for in letters from his mother which he had shown me she had always called him that—"this is very kind of you, but I think no. I think it's no good for you. You go back to America—" Here I am afraid I broke down and for the first time since the militiaman stopped me at the peasant market I cried.

He held me tightly and said some very sweet things, things that I shall always remember and cherish.

"Come on now, smile," he told me, "and promise me that you'll have faith. That you'll never give up. We'll win this yet."

"What does win mean?" I asked.

"Win," he replied, looking rather helpless. "Win, well, I don't know the word in Russian. You know, it's like pobeda."

"Pobeda? You mean victory?"

"Da, da"—he beamed—"we'll have a Russian-American pobeda."

"Pobeda over what?"

"That son-of-a-bitch Beria and his secret police," he said.

"What's son-off-beach?"

"Beria," he told me, giving me a big kiss.

7 I had been with my mother's cousin in her village home just one day when a man in the uniform of the NKVD arrived asking to see me.

"You must accompany me to Ryazan," he announced. Unprotestingly I went with him. This was not Moscow or anything like it. It was the deep country. The Germans were close by and apparently there was no automobile or gasoline to waste on me. We traveled the narrow dirt road in an ancient four-wheeled droshky.

This time the inquisitor was a colonel, a small, bald man with a fringe of thick black hair. His baldness accentuated a broad bulbous forehead halfway up which hung a pair of strange eyebrows. They were like two loops of licorice, and with his big knob of a head, his black staring eyes, thin arms that tapered into tiny restless hands, he looked to me like a black widow spider.

"Are you Tamara Adamovna Kolb-Chernashova?" he began.

I answered that I was.

"Give me your documents."

Turning them over with quick jerky gestures in his busy little fingers, he said, "There was some question of you going to Shadrinsk."

"But that was changed in Moscow."

"I'll do the talking, citizenness. You just answer my questions."

As in the Lubyanka there was a picture of Stalin on the

wall, but instead of the engraving of Lenin, here there was one of Beria behind the colonel's desk.

"You were directed to Ryazan, but the question of Shadrinsk has yet to be resolved, and until it is resolved you are restricted to your village. Do you understand me?"

The whine of an air-raid siren broke into his monologue.

"Boris, Boris," the colonel called out as he jumped to his feet, which I now saw were encased in a small pair of shiny black leather boots. They were very small boots but they were not small enough to encompass snugly his spindly little legs.

"Boris," he shouted, rushing to the door.

"Coming, Comrade Colonel."

Guns sounded outside. It was late evening and the lights went out.

"Put this one in a cell," called the colonel and in the dark I could hear him fleeing down the uncarpeted corridor outside his office.

"You," asked a voice, "where are you?"

"Here," said I from my chair.

I felt a hard hand on my shoulder. Dragging me to my feet the man half-led, half-pulled me down several corridors. Outside, all over Ryazan the antiaircraft guns chorused, "Boom-boom-boom-boom-boom." I heard the long-drawn-out whine of a bomb dropping, and then an explosion.

"In there," shouted the man, giving me such a push that I fell, striking one knee a sharp whack against something and ending up flat on a damp stone floor.

"Is there anyone here?" I called out.

There was no answer.

"Is there anyone here?"

Silence except for the din outside.

More bombs fell and by the light of the explosions I could see that I was in a cell—three stone walls and a door of steel bars. I saw dimly that what my knee had hit was a chair. In my predicament it seemed useless even to try to move, but I felt I must do something. I climbed on top of a small table and tried to look out of the high barred window. The building to which I had been brought was surrounded by a lofty board fence. Beyond this I could see the flashes of the antiaircraft guns. Soon a dull glow began to light up the sky, obviously from fires started by the bombs. Well, there was nothing I could do about it.

It was a long nightmarish ordeal, for the bombing continued spasmodically for several hours. Physically and emotionally exhausted, I fell asleep on top of the table. The sound of my door being opened awakened me the next morning. A man in a none too clean NKVD uniform handed me a cup of unsweetened strong tea. I presumed he must be the man from the night before.

"When you've finished, come with me," he said.

"I'd like to go to the ladies room."

"Ladies room? Ha!" he mocked. "Go in there." He pushed me into an evil-smelling enclosure. However filthy, it served my purpose.

Once more I was confronted by the spidery little colonel. He shuffled some papers on his desk and without referring to the bombing or his undignified exit the previous evening said, "As I have told you, your case has yet to be resolved. Until it has, return to your village and do not leave it. You understand?"

"Yes."

Boris was summoned and stood beside the colonel.

"How do I get back?" I asked.

"You walk," said the colonel.

"Walk?"

"Yes, walk. You don't look crippled to me, and don't you hang about in Ryazan. That's forbidden."

It was a gorgeous mild morning and the smell of freshly turned earth in the champagne-like air lifted my spirits as I walked along the country road, which was dusty and deeply rutted by wagon wheels. Some mile or two outside the city I saw a number of young soldiers off to one side of the road. Near them were several long-barreled artillery pieces that I took to be antiaircraft guns. The soldiers waved to me. I waved back but quickened my pace and kept my eyes straight ahead. I was in enough trouble already. I certainly did not need an additional accusation of carrying out military espionage.

My mother's cousin not only welcomed me back to the house but insisted on making me a tremendous breakfast of kasha, coffee, and real hen eggs.

"I have a surprise for you," she said. "This came yesterday, when you were away." She produced a large cardboard box and a letter.

"Who brought it?"

"A man in a foreign automobile."

"Who was he?"

"He didn't say. He only asked that I give these to you. He said you would understand."

"Was he a chauffeur?"

"I don't know, but he was Russian."

I did understand. The long beautiful letter in English with a Russian translation by his secretary was from Eddy. I still have it. I would quote from it, but some letters are too personal, too exquisitely intimate ever to make public. It was signed "Honey" and it is enough to say that it gave me great hope but also great fear. He said that there was nothing he could do in Russia to help me, but he felt things could be done in the United States if he saw certain people. He had had no vacation for nearly three years and there was an opportunity of getting back to America quickly. He planned to leave the first week in May.

Oh, God. He was going to put seven thousand miles between us.

"You must trust me and believe in me, my darling," he said, "and in the end, all will be well."

With a sinking heart I folded the letter and held it

tightly in both hands. I felt I must cling to it. It was the only
link that connected us.

"Aren't you going to open the box?" asked my cousin.

"Oh, yes."

It contained a badly needed pair of low-heeled shoes, a
pair of stockings, a dress, a sweater, several cans of food,
butter, and sugar. Where had he got them? I had no idea.

The box also contained a sealed envelope and inside
were five hundred-ruble notes. I held out the money to her.
"This is for you," I said. "For you and your husband who
have so kindly taken me in. I don't know when I'll get any
more of this. Please put it against my room and board."

Her reaction was furious and she lectured me at length on
the value of love and kindness. When she finished I stammered out my thanks and kissed her. She took me in her
arms and, rocking me as if I were a baby, hummed an old
lullaby I had known as a child.

"Money," she muttered. "How dare you think I'd take
your money. You'll need it, dushka."

8 A week dragged by and again I was wanted in Ryazan. This time a pair of NKVD men called for me in a wagon. It was late afternoon and my visits seemed destined to be coupled with air raids, for as we neared the antiaircraft emplacement south of the city, I heard the sound of a low-flying plane. The driver whipped up the horse and as he did two soldiers walking beside the road hopped into the back near where I was sitting on a rough sack on the bed of the wagon. One of the soldiers—I think he was a sergeant—ordered the driver, "Get us to our station as quickly as you can. Now make that horse move."

"Where's your station?"

"Up ahead. Don't ask questions, comrade. Make that horse go faster."

We traveled about a half mile when a gray-colored plane jumped out of the skies with its cannon and machine guns blasting away.

"Down, down," shouted the young noncommissioned officer, pushing me flat. The antiaircraft guns opened up. Our driver pulled up the horse and he and the other NKVD man jumped out and scrambled for a ditch, leaving me with the two soldiers.

"Come on," ordered the sergeant, tugging me out of the wagon. Why the horse did not panic I do not know, but with all the shouting and shooting, he began calmly nibbling away at grass alongside the road.

Somehow my situation seemed hilariously ridiculous. Here I was being taken to NKVD headquarters for more questioning—or worse—by two grown men, while two other men seemed bent on protecting me. Instead of following my new-found protectors, I just stood still in the middle of the dusty road and began laughing. Once started I could not stop.

"What's the matter with you, girl?" demanded the sergeant.

"It's all so funny," I fairly screamed. "I'm a political prisoner. Do you understand that? I'm a political prisoner and you're trying to save me."

I felt a sharp slap. My face stung. Next I was being shaken by the shoulders.

"Come to your senses. Get a grip on yourself. You're hysterical."

Grabbing me by a wrist he ran with me to a slit trench and pulled me in with him. All this happened very quickly. As we lay in the trench, the nearby guns pounding away, the sergeant said, "Forgive me for hitting you, but you were going to pieces."

Calmer now, I said, "But I *am* a political prisoner."

He smiled and began laughing. I joined him. Like a pair of idiots we lay there roaring at one another.

"I don't know what's happened to my guards," I said when I got control of myself.

"Guards? Are you serious?"

"Yes."

"They're in those other trenches. Just stay where you are. We'll hide you from them."

"Thank you, I'm in enough trouble already. You're kind, but I mustn't get involved with the military."

He looked at me very strangely. I am sure he thought I was crazy.

"Is it safe to get up?"

"You'd better stay for a few minutes more."

We lay there saying nothing. The guns were quiet at last. In a few minutes he stood up and looked around.

"It's all right now."

Climbing out of the trench, I saw that the horse was still grazing beside the road, but there was no sign of my captors.

"Here I am," I shouted, "over here."

About fifty yards away on the other side of the road they slowly emerged from their trench. I told the soldiers good-bye, thanked them and returned to the wagon. Without speaking we rumbled on to Ryazan where once more I was brought before the spider man.

"You received a parcel from Moscow," he began. "We could seize it, you know."

I made no comment.

"It was from the American?"

"Yes."

"I see. All right, you can keep it."

"Thank you."

"About Shadrinsk, the question is still unresolved."

"But can't I remain here?"

"That remains to be seen. You don't deserve any favors, you know."

"I know."

"Well, that's all for now. You may return to your village."

I made the trip again on foot.

Ten or more days staggered by, and Meester Gilmore's letters dictated to his secretary in English and translated into Russian—so there could be no possibility of a mis-understanding—said his plans were now worked out. He would leave Moscow sometime during the first part of May. For security reasons, somebody else's not his, he emphasized, he did not know the exact date.

The fact that he was really going back to his homeland now hit me like a delayed shock. Could he, or he and I together, ever surmount the obstacles ahead? If he reached America would the Soviet authorities ever let him return? Was my final destination to be Shadrinsk? Could I survive it? Was there anything he could do in America? These and a hundred more questions nagged me during the long days and nights of village life. But above all else I could not let him go without saying farewell. Would it really be farewell? Russians avoid the formality and finality of farewell, preferring "Dos vadanaya," or "Till we meet again." I still had hope but I wanted desperately to see him once more. One night I made up my mind and whispered to my cousin what I hoped to do. I asked her if she could arrange for me to go into Ryazan the following day in one of the villager's wagons. She saw to this and as dusk was falling across the broad fields I hid myself under some sacks and was on my way.

Getting to Moscow from Ryazan was a big undertaking, for in those war years everyone had to possess a stamped permit to travel. This was only half-solving things, though. On presentation of the travel documents their owner hoped to be issued a railway ticket. Then, assuming the ticket was forthcoming, one had to find a place on the few and crowded trains.

I realized I had no chance of getting a travel permit. Desperation finds its way and I simply hitchhiked by train. Sometimes I clung to the steps of the packed passenger cars. I was not alone. About twenty others, some young, some middle-aged, and some old, were traveling by the same forbidden route and I reasoned that I had a fair chance of eluding the railway police, the militia, and the military police strung out along the railway line. I did what the others did. I would drop from my perilous perch as the train slowed down for the towns, and merge with the shadows.

The towns were all blacked out, so we simply trotted along in the dark, unseen we hoped, beside the train. When it stopped we stopped. When it moved off we rushed back to the steps and the spaces between the coaches. These spaces, above the big steel couplings, were more dangerous than the steps but they had a certain advantage. They were more sheltered than the open steps and not so cold.

I spent two nights in such travel and reached Moscow famished and exhausted about dawn on May 3. The Ryazansky Vauxzal was not too far from my mother's apartment, which I made for on foot. Should I dare telephone Eddy at his little house on Ulitsa Shchukina so early in the morning? Why not? On the way to my mother's I crept into a public telephone booth and dialed Arbat 6 5055. It rang for an eternity and then I recognized the voice of his old servant, Pasha.

"May I speak to Gospodin Gilmore?" I asked without identifying myself.

"He's not here. He's gone."

I did not drop the receiver, but my heart dropped.

"Where's he gone?"

"He's gone to America."

"When did he go?"

"Yesterday morning."

Alas, I was too late.

"Do you know when he's coming back?"

"In two or three months." In two or three months where would I be?

"Thank you," I said and I am afraid I began to cry.

My mother was delighted but at the same time terribly frightened at seeing me.

"You shouldn't have dared," she told me amid our kisses. "This'll be terrible for you if you're seen here."

"I had to see him."

"Yes, darling," she comforted me. "I understand, I understand, but I'm sure you must get back as quickly as you can."

Returning to Ryazan was not quite as difficult as getting to Moscow had been. Still, it was hitchhiking—Russian style. Feeling myself a veteran I made for my favorite perch on the couplings. This time the journey took less time, for I seemed to have attached myself to a train that was transporting factory machinery and workers eastward. We reached Ryazan early one morning and for the third time I walked to my village. The relief was sweet when I discovered I had had no callers.

Two weeks and more passed and then I did have visitors. This time they arrived in an automobile.

"Tamara Adamovna," said an NKVD officer whose face was new to me, "how are you getting along here?"

"Very well," I replied. The unexpected solicitude baffled me. Was it the smile before the frown? The caress before the kick? Was I, at last, bound for Shadrinsk?

"Are you well?"

"Perfectly well, thank you."

"Well enough to travel?"

Was he taunting me?

"Yes," I said.

"How would you like to go back to Moscow?"

I felt I should be cautious. Perhaps this was a trick.

"Then get your things together, Tamara Adamovna. You're going home."

I dared not ask if he meant home to Moscow and a cell in the Lubyanka, or home to Ulitsa Krasina.

"Just give me a couple of minutes, please."

"Of course."

I could hardly believe what I was hearing. Was I dreaming?

On the trip to Ryazan the officer and his friend, a man in plainclothes, could not have been more friendly. They rode in the front seat and left the rear one to me and my pitiful bag of possessions. This seating arrangement in itself was a subtle difference in prisoner-jailer relationship. As they were in the front seat and I on the back seat, they were not guarding me.

Instead of proceeding to what I presumed was their headquarters—the place where I spent the night during the air raid—I was taken directly to the railway station.

"Wait here in the car," the officer said. "I'll see about your documents."

I thought it best to ask no questions, so I waited, making small talk with the plainclothesman who drove. Surprisingly, the officer returned fairly soon.

"Here is your travel permit," he said, "and here is your ticket. I'm afraid the train is not due for another two hours. Would you like some tea?"

"Thank you, yes."

The whole business mystified me and when the train did arrive the officer not only saw me to the train, but also found me a seat and told everyone within hearing that I was not to be disturbed.

"I hope you have a pleasant trip."

"Thank you, and thank you for your kindness."

Saluting me, he turned and left. I traveled in comfort and in such a daze that I cannot, for the life of me, remember anything about that journey, whether it took one day or two, how I ate or who my companions may have been.

On the other hand, I recall quite well being met at the railway station in Moscow by two officers in a uniform I was getting used to. Extremely polite, they inquired after my health and said they had an automobile waiting to take me home.

A tiny but real fear gnawed at me. Was this, even at the last moment, some ghastly hoax? I knew that the Russian wife of a British correspondent, in possession of an exit visa, was once removed from a Teheran-bound train at Baku and kept waiting for hours uncertain if the doors of the frontier were being slammed shut in her face. On another occasion the Polish-born wife of an American was, after much petitioning, granted an exit visa to Poland, then taken from her railway carriage a few kilometers before the Soviet-Polish boundary. So far as I know and her husband knows, she never reached Poland. Under mounting pressure by the State Department some organ of the Stalin Government later informed the husband that his missing wife had "died of natural causes some years ago."

These things and others crowded my mind as the two officers and I rumbled away from the railway station. So great was my apprehension that as the car reached a certain intersection I hardly breathed. Would the car turn to the left? If it did, this would mean the route to the Lubyanka. A turn to the right would be the way home.

It turned to the right.

On this occasion I did not ask to be put out of the car before we reached my mother's apartment house. This time it did not matter and I felt sure that it would not matter to my mother either—for I was home.

Since leaving my village I had been in the company of four officers of the NKVD, yet not one of them explained or even commented upon the fact of my release.

Only months later did I learn the explanation of my miracle.

Eddy Gilmore had called on his good friend Wendell Willkie, told him the whole story and asked Willkie personally to intervene with Stalin.

A few days after my return to Moscow I received a cable from Eddy. It said:

PLEASE CONFIRM BY CABLE THAT YOU ARE NOW HOME IN MOSCOW STOP MY ADDRESS TIME BEING ASSOCIATED PRESS WASHINGTON STOP ALL MY LOVE HONEY.

With lifting heart I confirmed.

Two days later the following cable was delivered to our door:

WELCOME HOME STOP I SHALL SEE YOU SOON IN MOSCOW NEVER TO BE SEPARATED AGAIN STOP MY DEAREST LOVE HONEY.

Only in his timing was he too optimistic. He assumed he would return to his Moscow post in a United States Air Force plane, at least as far as Teheran. The war was still very much on, however, and a foreign correspondent on his way to the USSR held no high travel priority. Instead of plane, he moved by train from Washington to Charleston, S.C., and after a few days there with his aunt and uncle, Mr. and Mrs. Ernest Chisholm, boarded a huge convoy for Suez via Norfolk. At Suez he rode a British truck into Cairo and there found himself in luck, luck in the pleasant shape of Gilmore Nunn, a transport officer of the American Armed Forces. Gilmore Nunn, like Eddy Gilmore, an alumnus of Washington and Lee University, got Meester Gilmore quickly to Teheran and from the Iranian capital Eddy flew in a Soviet plane to Moscow.

To say that I met him at the Moscow Airport seems one of the great understatements of my life. I enveloped him at Moscow Airport.

When Mr. Willkie asked Generalissimo Stalin—as a personal favor—to have me released from police confinement, he also pointed out that Eddy's employers wanted to send him back to his post so that he could continue his coverage of the Red Army's struggle against the German Army and the no less courageous war effort of the Soviet people.

At the end of a long cable that Mr. Willkie dispatched to Stalin he also mentioned that it was Eddy's hope to marry me and he would deeply appreciate it if the Generalissimo would assist in making this possible.

The whole audacious appeal worked.

The wedding took place through our friend and interpreter Madame Tchechova before, of all things, a tribunal of three officials and a large audience of members of the Moscow Soviet. We were married in a large room in a building that would correspond to a city hall in a big American city. We listened to a speech in Russian on Russian-American peaceful co-existence by a brown-haired female official. That the wedding took place at such an exalted Soviet level I can only ascribe to the intervention of Joseph Stalin and Wendell Willkie, with heavy emphasis on Willkie.

Earlier I said that Americans are tremendously kind. I repeat it.

9 To sum up:

Because of my love for an American I was banished from my Moscow home. While it was true that the United States and the Soviet Union were allies in the war against Hitler, at best theirs was a shaky, uneasy alliance with deep suspicion on both sides.

During all my conscious life teachers and instructors drummed into my brain that capitalist America was my homeland's implacable foe, that ideologically and politically they were as incompatible as vinegar and milk, or honey and bath water, yet here was I wed to one of these Americans, and a rather conservative one at that. He was no admirer of socialism, let alone Communism, and in Moscow, the self-professed citadel of Marxism, he made no secret of his strong views.

Enthusiastic in praise of the Russian people, he maintained that if they were ever allowed to think, write, compose, paint, and speak with complete freedom, they would out-distance all other creative peoples of the world.

Honey and bath water? My husband and I had totally dissimilar backgrounds.

He was born in a small southern town of Scotch-Irish ancestors who less than one hundred years before owned slaves. He was also a practicing Christian.

On the other hand, my background was wholly urban and proletarian. I was neither a Communist nor a member of the young Communist league. Politics bored me then almost as much as they bore me now, which is to say a very

great deal—yet it was a politician who ended my banishment from Moscow and made my marriage possible. My
ancestors were Slavic and certainly one branch had been
serfs. My religion was Russian Orthodox. Although I had
grown up under a system that denied God, my mother remained deeply religious, kept ikons about her and still does,
and while I seldom attended any religious service in Moscow,
I considered myself a Christian, admittedly not a very good
one.

In marrying an American I realized that I was doing
something very different, that I was setting myself apart
from friends and perhaps family. If I realized all this I am
afraid I gave no serious thought to what could be the
inherent dangers in an American-Soviet alliance such as
my husband's and mine. When one is in love one does not
become preoccupied with such things. If I ever thought of
them they gave me no worry.

As the Russian wife of an American I lived from 1943 to
1953 in Moscow—ten long and difficult but in many ways
very happy years. Two of our children, Victoria Wendell
and Susanna Hager were born in Russia. They came into life
as dual nationals, the Soviet authorities recognizing them as
Soviet citizens by fact of a Russian mother. The United
States Government looked on Vicki and Susanna as Americans because of their father's nationality.

Together, Eddy and I watched the uneasy wartime alliance of the USSR and its western allies sour into a heavily
armed peace, both sides more suspicious of the other than
ever. With the proclamation of the Truman Doctrine in
1947, the already frosty atmosphere of the cold war froze
solid. Diplomatic relations between America and Russia
underwent a severe strain. I lost my Russian friends, many
of whom I had known since childhood. I was given a wide
berth. People I had known for years turned their heads
when we passed one another on the streets, frightened lest
they be seen speaking to me.

Beria's secret police intruded once more, this time warning my mother that she, my sister, and my brother should no longer visit the Gilmore residence. "It's a dangerous house," they told her.

My sister, who had a good job as a secretary to a deputy minister in a department that dealt with nothing more military than food, lost her job. In those days, and for all I know now, job applicants filled out long forms which asked many questions about the job-seekers' backgrounds. One of the questions was, "Do you have any foreigners among your relatives?"

To this my sister truthfully put down Eddy's name as her brother-in-law. She promptly lost her job, was dismissed from at least two others, and was without work for five months until some courageous official in the Moscow Gas Company took her on. More terrible than this persecution, however, was the case of her husband.

In the early days of the cold war she met and became engaged to a young naval officer. As an aide to an admiral he held a relatively important job and one which certainly involved security.

While Beria's police put our house out-of-bounds to my Russian relatives, nothing had been said about my visiting them and I did this quite regularly. One day my sister told me about her naval officer and, of course, I mentioned the engagement to Eddy. I was jolted by his reaction.

"Congratulate them," he said, "but I don't want to meet the young man. No, that's not right. I would like to meet him, but I know it wouldn't be right."

"I think he wants to meet you," I said. "After all, you're going to be brothers-in-law."

"I can't help that. We must never meet."

"Why not?"

"Can't you see?" he asked impatiently. "He's in the armed forces. More than that he's an aide to an admiral. By knowing me he'd become a security risk. No, I don't want to see him and I won't see him."

They never met, yet shortly after his marriage to Zina, Alexei disappeared. He was last seen by my sister as he stepped aboard a Murmansk-bound train in Moscow. In a matter of a few weeks she was to have followed him.

When no letters or communication of any kind arrived from him she began worrying. She sent him a telegram. It was unanswered. She followed up with letters. Becoming desperate she tried to reach him by telephone. He was always unavailable. After weeks of this the wife of another naval officer whispered she had heard that Alexei was under arrest. By letter, telephone, and personal visits to the Armed Forces Ministry, Zina tried to establish what had happened to her husband. She got nowhere. The poor girl was almost out of her mind. Only months after her husband's disappearance was she able to confirm that he had been arrested, tried, and convicted on a charge of "lack of revolutionary vigilance." He had married a Soviet citizen whose sister was married to an American. His crime was no small one, for his sentence was eight years.

Quite naturally this had the most depressing effect on Eddy and me. He felt deeply responsible for Alexei's tragic predicament as he had felt responsible for my arrest.

Just after this calamity my husband's two secretaries disappeared. From their relatives we learned what had happened. To begin with, both Lydia and Alicia had been given permission to work for him and The Associated Press. With their appointment registered with the Soviet authorities, they were now taken into custody for performing the very duties the Government originally had approved. How far would this madness go? Would they next expel my husband? It had happened to others.

The expulsion of a correspondent followed a pattern. First his secretary or secretaries were arrested. In time a denunciation of him by the secretary appeared in the Soviet press. Usually he was accused of being a spy. You can imagine our state of mind as we waited for the inevitable.

Enough of this, though. Meester Gilmore was not denounced in the press by his secretaries, but we both felt he came very close to trouble. Soon after, a Soviet-dominated country of eastern Europe tried to embarrass a big American news agency by arresting one of Eddy's colleagues. We both felt it could have been Eddy instead.

I could fill pages with recitations of the bouts of political pneumonia brought on by the chilling blizzards of the cold war, but I think everyone knows about them.

Since Stalin's death, even Soviet writers have been turning out moving accounts of wholesale persecutions in lurid detail; of how no one was safe with the exception of Stalin, and haunted as he was by his grotesque fears and suspicions, he too became a prisoner, a prisoner of his own paranoia.

Then Stalin died, and I suppose we shall never know all about that. At the time, a flood of rumors swept Moscow, nearly all of them melodramatic. Before it is too late, it seems to me that his closest associates should agree on just what did take place in Moscow on those windy, wild days of early March 1953.

I know one thing that happened. The Gilmore family was allowed to leave the Soviet Union.

A few months after Stalin's demise, Mr. Charles E. Bohlen, then American Ambassador in Moscow, was called to Foreign Minister V. M. Molotov's office and informed that my application for an exit visa would be granted. Our long wait was over.

At this point I would like to emphasize that Stalin would have been delighted at my husband's departure any time, but had he left Russia without the children and me, I feel certain that he would never have seen us again, and I shall always be thankful to The Associated Press for letting him remain at his Moscow post. As he worked under the harshest and most frustrating of censorships, his reports hardly electrified the world's press, or greatly contributed to an understanding of what was really going on in Russia, controlled as it was then by one of the most formidable mass murderers in history.

Living in Russia in those days was not easy for foreigners. I know of two who had to be removed from Moscow in straitjackets, yet when they had arrived they were perfectly sane. How my husband was able to live and work under the pressures and anxieties that became his daily lot, I do not know. He said he was able to do it because he took refuge in a jazz band. They called themselves The Kremlin Krows and they made pretty good music. Even with his escape into music I still cannot understand how he stayed at his post for eleven years and nine months and still retained his sense of humor. But then again, there is the American husband for you. I consider them rather special.

10 Before I, as a Soviet citizen, could enter the United States with my American husband and my two children with their dual nationality, there were many formalities to complete. The American authorities in Stockholm were ever so kind and I got myself documented in about a month.

As we had shipped our car from Moscow ahead of us, it was waiting in Sweden, a huge Packard with special springs for negotiating Russian cobblestones. From Stockholm we drove leisurely to Paris, stopping with hospitable friends along the way.

Paris! Paris in early summer. I had never imagined any city could be so beautiful and this includes Leningrad by moonlight. As Eddy in Sweden had engaged an English-speaking nurse for the children, I had lots of time to enjoy the full charm of one of the world's most delightful capitals.

In pre-Communist days and since, Paris has been a spiritual Mecca for many Russians. It was certainly that for this one. After Paris came a delightfully smooth Atlantic crossing in a ship, the memory of which I shall always love, the old *Île de France*.

Aboard we found ourselves sitting at the captain's table, but with no disrespect for the *Île*'s master, the most interesting man at that table was an Englishman with a long nose, pink complexion, and eyes the color of skimmed milk. A complete color contrast to his wife, he was light and pastel, while she was dark olive with flashing black eyes and an outrageous sense of humor. They were Sir William

Walton, the distinguished composer, and his Argentine-born wife, Susanna. Since that crossing they have remained our devoted and most helpful friends. The trouble is they now live on Ischia, and that is a long way from almost any place.

Our arrival in New York was hectic.

My husband had always told me that newspapermen were not news. He was wrong as he often was.

We spent six straight hours in being interviewed and photographed. When I complained to Eddy that the children and I were tired, he said, "What do you think these newspaper and television people are up to, enjoying a holiday?"

"I don't understand you."

"Don't you realize that these people are doing a job? I'm sure they had much rather be back in their homes or with their friends some place than interviewing us. Come on now, let's help them all we can. I mean—smile."

"But why are they so interested in us?"

"Because we've become a fairly well-known family."

"But we haven't done anything to deserve all this attention."

He swelled himself up like an outsized balloon. "The hell we haven't. I've outlasted Joe Stalin and at my age and weight that's something."

"But what have we done?"

"Some day you'll understand. We have done something that few people in this world have done. We have outwaited, outwitted, and outlasted Stalin, and he was one of the great waiters of all time. We've beaten him at his waiting game. One day you'll understand that few people, however passively, overcame Stalin at anything. So, for God's sake please keep on smiling and looking pretty."

In New York I spent some time in the company of five unusual and dissimilar men—Kent Cooper, Colonel Robert McCormick, Eddie Condon, John Steinbeck, and Joe Bushkin.

Then general manager of The Associated Press, Mr. Cooper was one of those unusual men whose life proved that music and journalism can be as compatible as ham and eggs. Although I have never had the pleasure of meeting him, Mr. Frank Sinatra is another, for was he not once a sports writer? In his tiny way, my husband was also a words-and-music man.

Not only did Mr. Cooper play the piano, but he also composed light popular music. His "Dixie Girl" was even recorded. He was an executive with strong likes and dislikes and luckily Eddy Gilmore, was not one of the dislikes. I think it always appealed to Mr. Cooper that while my husband was his chief of bureau in Moscow, he rented a handsome Bechstein piano from the Soviet Government and entered it on his monthly expense account as an office radio, and was courageous enough, or stupid enough, to explain the arrangement to the general manager. Mr. Cooper seemed to treat the matter as a musical conspiracy in which he, as the AP's general manager, was called on to play his part. I mean month-in, month-out to O.K. that office radio.

Lest I create the wrong impression, I think I should get something straight—Eddy Gilmore was no musician. As he said, he could fake a bit on several instruments while really playing none of them. He was a pretty good blues singer, though, and to his accompaniment on the balalaika startled many a Russian with a rendition of "Empty Bed Blues" and "Back O' Town Blues." He knew many jazz musicians and held them as a race apart from other mortals. I had spent a great many hours of my life in various parts of the world watching him enjoy jazz and the men who play it. Time and again I had heard them invite him to join them on the bandstand and he had always refused, with the logical explanation that he did not perform in front of professional musicians, that he had too much respect for their art form. Yet, thinking back, there have been exceptions; singing a duet with Louis Armstrong, as Satchmo, his delightful wife

Lucille, Eddy, and I sat on the floor of the maestro's carpeted suite in Geneva's Hotel du Rhone in the dawn of a summer Saturday. Louis insisted on drinking Cherry Heering as he and Eddy sang "Old Rockin' Chair." On another occasion in Geneva we spent the evening with Edmond Hall, the clarinet player, and after Marie closed the bar, an impromptu session was held, my husband drumming softly on a suitcase with wire brushes as Edmond played some of his most glorious tunes. Oh, yes, the Rumanian pianist stayed up and tinkled away to what I am sure was the best clarinet and the worst drums he ever accompanied.

Colonel McCormick was no musician as far as I know. Anyhow, the evening Mr. Cooper and his lovely Sally took us to dinner with the Colonel and Mrs. McCormick, music would have been superfluous. I hardly understood a word they said but there were a great many words. I am not sure how the general manager of The Associated Press ever persuaded the publisher even to sit at the same table with me, with his strong views on the Soviet Union, a country on whose passport I was still traveling. But he did, and the Colonel seemed to go out of his way to talk to me. I do not think I understood a word he said, and perhaps this is just as well. In our hotel room Eddy asked me what I thought of Colonel McCormick.

"Well, at least he doesn't have horns, which, after some of the things I've heard, comes as a surprise."

"A lot of people don't like him," said Eddy, "but I'll say this for him, he puts out a hell of a good newspaper. I may not agree with all his editorials, but when news happens— I mean the big story—the Chicago *Tribune* really covers it."

As for Mr. Condon: My husband always said that he was one of the most articulate men in America. I am too inarticulate to speak on articulation, but I think Mr. Condon is one of the dearest men anywhere.

Despite his consideration for other people, he is very

unkind to himself, for I have never met anyone who seems to be so consistently plagued with hangovers. He is one of America's outstanding authorities on the subject. His cure is classic.

"For a hangover," says Eddie, "take the juice of a quart of whisky."

Conversationally, he has never accepted today's fifth of a gallon measure. With him it always is a quart.

I first met him in our hotel where he appeared one midday with my husband, Joe Bushkin, and a hangover. Small and then in his late forties, he is the youngest-looking grown man I have ever seen. Now in his sixties, he owns all of his hair and teeth. He has a warm-hearted and witty wife named Phyllis, who is almost too smart for a wife. The Condons have two lovely daughters, and Liza—the one I know the best—looks like her father, minus a hangover. A doting father, Eddie nevertheless seems uneasy in the company of young children. My husband said this was because they reminded him of "the little people." What did he mean by this? He refused to explain. In our hotel Mr. Condon and Mr. Bushkin, a fine piano player, made the right noises to our children.

I found the pair of hung-over musicians fascinating. Both are virtuosos, of course, so I suppose I have made a mistake in referring to them as musicians. It is a bit like referring to Georges Auguste Escoffier as a cook, or to the Beatles as hairy young men.

During that lively New York afternoon, Mr. Condon paid me what I consider the finest compliment ever to come my way—and at the time I did not know what he was talking about.

Speaking to Professor Bushkin, and nodding toward me, he said, "Tamara—just look at her. Why that Gilmore's got an egg in his beer."

This remark greatly confused me, for I thought he said,

"Tamara has put an egg in Gilmore's beer." It seemed very crazy because Eddy does not drink beer.

During that same stay in New York I met John Steinbeck for the second time. My first introduction to the Nobel Prize winner was in Moscow years before when he was on a visit to the Soviet Union trying to spend the rubles accumulated in his name as royalties earned by the publication—without the author's consent—of at least one of his novels. In those days I had only the vaguest idea who he was. At a late party at our house he wrote a poem for me saying, "That's the only poem I've ever written in my life." Unfortunately I misplaced the poem and am unable to remember what it was about. How I would like to have it now. Years later when I told my husband about the lost Steinbeck poem, he thought for a moment and asked:

"You're sure you can't remember anything about it?"

"Nothing."

"You are certain that you don't even know what it was about?"

"Certain."

"Then that's fine."

"Why is it fine? I think it would be wonderful to remember something about the first poem such a great writer wrote."

"No, it's better this way."

"Why? I don't understand."

"Because as things stand, it is now impossible for you or anyone else to blackmail John for a Moscow indiscretion."

One day in New York, John took my husband to what must be one of the world's longest lunches. I stayed at the hotel looking after the children. The meal, at John's favorite restaurant, commenced at 1 P.M. and they did not get up until just after 7 P.M.

"Yes, John," said Eddy, "the food *is* good here, but you must know several places where it's just as good."

"I like it for more than the food," said John. "I repeat, this is the best restaurant in the world."

"But why?"

"Well, I'll tell you. No matter what time I come here, no matter how early or how late, I can always get a clean shirt, a girl, or a football ticket."

11 In Russia, Eddy had been working for years without a vacation, so the AP gave him a long one in the United States. We spent most of it at his Alabama home. We arrived at night and all I could see was a town built on the high bank of a large river, but that next morning, oh dear.

I woke up to a medley of soft voices and the song of many birds outside the house. Peeping through a window I looked out on the intersection of two wide streets, over which trees formed long and deep arches. I saw seven human beings, all of them Negroes, and not one of them was moving. One leaned on a rake talking to a friend who sat a-straddle a bicycle. In what appeared to be our front garden a slim man in overalls leaned against a tree talking to a pretty girl in a bright red dress. Farther up the street was an old automobile with no top and in the front seat sat a fat man with very white teeth. He seemed to be waiting for someone. A tall man, the color of a cigar, stood on a strip of strawlike grass, between a broad sidewalk and the street proper, and he seemed to be talking to the fat man in the car, but the fat man neither looked at him nor seemed to pay him any attention. Over to the left was another man in dark trousers and a white shirt. He stood stock-still, but in one hand he held a rubber hose and from it flowed a thin stream of water. He looked like a fountain statue. I turned back to the man closest to the window, the one with the rake. He had not moved, and as far as I could tell, neither had

the others. Except for the fat man with the white teeth all
seemed to be smiling or laughing.

"What wonderful-looking people," I thought.

I reached out and touched my husband's shoulder.

"Good morning," I greeted him. "Look outside. Do you see
what I see?"

"Good morning. I don't know what you see."

"Look—there are seven people. Count them. And not one
of them's moving."

Eddy glanced through the window and then slumped back
on his pillow. "It's too hot to move," he said. "You can't
expect anyone to work in this heat."

"Why are they all laughing?"

"Are they laughing?"

"Those who aren't laughing out loud—listen, you can
hear them—those who aren't laughing are smiling. It's the
same thing."

"If they're laughing and smiling, then I reckon it's because they're happy, but unless things have changed a lot,
they don't have a hell of a lot to happy about."

"Why not?"

"It's a long story."

"But I'd like to know."

"Listen, my Russkie bride, promise me one thing, you
won't start making up your mind about things down here
in Selma until you've been here a great deal longer than you
have."

"Why?"

"Well, just take my word, please."

"Where are all the white people? Are they asleep?"

"A lot of them are—if they've got any sense—but don't
believe everything your eyes see down here, and don't
believe everything your eyes don't see."

"I don't understand."

"I hope you will one day."

"But all the white people can't be asleep."

"I can assure you that they aren't. Why, every farmer for miles around—white and black—has been up for hours."

"I don't know why I haven't asked you about the South before. Please tell me all about it."

"Do you remember a very nice woman I once mentioned named Margaret Mitchell? We used to work on the same newspaper. When you are really reading well in English, I want you to read a book she wrote. It'll tell you a lot about the Deep South. You read that book and then when I am sure that you understand everything you read in English, I want you to read something else—"

"What's that?"

"A speech Mr. Lincoln made."

"Who was Mr. Lincoln?"

"A President of the United States."

"All right, Honey, I'll read Margaret Mitchell's book and Mr. Lincoln's speech."

"You do," he said, "and then I think you'll know a lot about the subject down here. And promise me one thing?"

"What's that?"

"That you won't talk to me any more about it until you do."

"I thought this was a free country, and that any citizen can talk about anything he wants to."

"That's just the point. You're not a citizen of this country—yet."

Aside from the heat of late summer I reveled in my first experience of really living in the United States, that land of such plenty.

The stores were packed with the most marvelous things. I was truly in a fairyland and in the beginning I actually thought for a few moments that everything was being given away because I never saw my husband paying for anything. He was charging his purchases, of course, but how was I to know about that?

My first shopping was for clothes for the children, and how simple it was. From what seemed to be a whole world of clothes I would pick what I wanted, and then Eddy would say to the always smiling saleslady, "She'll have this one, please."

Whatever I bought—shoes, socks, dresses, playsuits, and the most beautiful underwear imaginable—the people in the shops would wrap it up, hand it over, and say, "Thank you."

They thanked *me*. What a country!

As far as I could tell, everything was free. This must be the pure Communism that Lenin said would one day prevail in the Soviet Union after we had passed through the Socialist phase.

Alas, the credit system had not yet been explained to me. That my husband must eventually pay for all those lovely things that I selected with such joy really never entered my mind.

Another pleasant surprise was the supermarket and the staggering abundance of food. But here, I observed, my husband paid. He showed me the prices and together we translated them into rubles. I discovered that I could buy twenty lemons in the American supermarket for the price I had paid for just one lemon in Moscow, and what about those steaks, cut and displayed so tastefully, and all the soap I could carry?

"This is, well, it's a sort of heaven," I told my husband.

"What?"

"All this plenty, this abundance, the stores that simply bulge with the most marvelous things, and to think they encourage you to buy them and take them away."

At that time we were living in a precious bungalow that Alice and Charles Hohenberg turned over to us in Selma.

"Come, sit down, I want to explain something to you," said Eddy.

I looked out a big window toward the west. Before us stretched fields of corn and cotton, and a soft breeze blew across them from a great wall of tall pines in the distance.

"You've now really been shopping. Now I'm putting this very simply—this is capitalism in operation."

"Then I'm certainly for it."

"So am I, and let's neither of us ever forget it. But I've got to explain several things to you. You're the mother of two children but you're still very young. You have been pitched from one sort of world smack into another sort of world. Capitalism, the system of free enterprise, is far to be recommended over any other system I've ever seen and any you're likely to see. However, I do want to point out to you that Russia and most of the countries of Europe have gone through two terrible wars in my lifetime. England lost a whole generation of young men in World War I and I don't think it's ever recovered. Russia and France and Germany lost millions, and Russia almost committed suicide by a revolution and a civil war. Then there's that Second World War, and you saw enough of it to know how terrible it was. Well, to put it very simply, America has not been fought over during two terrible wars. Its cities were not bombed. Its mankind wasn't bled white. Just remember these basic facts the next time you visit the supermarket. This is a new country. Its land is not exhausted by centuries of over-farming."

"All right," I told him, "I get the point."

"And another thing, capitalism and the American way of life aren't perfect. Far from it."

"I know. Those slums we drove through around New York, Newark, Philadelphia, Washington, Richmond, and Atlanta, and . . . well, here."

"You've got a lot to see and to learn," he said, putting his arm around me and kissing me gently on the cheek.

"I'm sorry, Honey. I'm not really as silly as I seem. I know that to have all this plenty, somebody's got to work for it and work very hard."

"That's one thing you'll learn about Americans. Most of them don't mind working."

"Why is this? Most people *do* mind working. Why are Americans different?"

"We don't have a monopoly on work, but I think we work harder than most people."

"But why?"

"I suppose it must be the system of free enterprise. There's no limit on how far a man can go in America."

"But this doesn't hold good for everyone."

"In theory it does, but in practice of course it doesn't. You've got me there, but I do want to say this, it's truer here than in any other country I know."

Here I should emphasize that I was just as naïve as I sound. When I left Russia I spoke very little English and had read no books in English.

Years before, as I commenced meeting Americans in Moscow, I began rejecting many of the things I had been taught in Joseph Stalin's schools about them and their country, so when I arrived in New York I was very confused about America. I was inclined to accept everything at face value, to believe what I saw with my own eyes, and I was seeing a new planet.

For Americans who have grown up in their country my outlook at the time of which I write must be difficult to accept. Encountering a capitalist society after growing up in a completely different world can give one a curious set of values. I cite a special one, a Russian girl friend. Moscow-born, she too had married a foreigner. Because of the war and his duties as an army officer, he was transferred from Moscow just after the wedding, and his Russian wife was not allowed to leave with him. She remained behind but was given two rooms within an embassy compound and was treated by the officers of her husband's mission just as if she had been a citizen of their country. This meant that among other privileges she received clothes packages from her husband. She was a very pretty girl and looked unusually beautiful in her new western clothes. She would have been a standout anywhere, but in the austerity of wartime Moscow many a Muscovite head turned to look at her in admiration as she walked by.

After a year or more of living alone in Russia she was finally granted an exit visa and left to join her husband in Canada via a boat trip to the United States.

On her first morning in America, she walked down a busy street in Baltimore's shopping center with two western friends she had known in Moscow. The longer she walked and the more people she saw the more silent she became. In Baltimore she was just another pretty face in the crowd. She turned no heads as she had turned them in her homeland. She churned up no gasps of admiration.

Ten minutes of this and she stopped, raised her hands to her face and burst into tears.

"But what on earth's the matter?" asked the wife of the couple accompanying her.

"It's so awful here," she sobbed. "Here in America everyone has pretty clothes. I can't stand it. I look like everyone else."

I thought of her as my American husband gave me that very elementary talk on capitalist America.

12 "You know," said my husband just before Christmas, "I'm supposed to be a foreign correspondent—"

"Well, you are, aren't you?" I told him more than asked.

"If I am I'd better get foreign again."

"Get foreign?"

"Yes. This is all very pleasant, you know, but I'm itchy."

"Itchy?"

"I suppose you'd call it my conscience, my old Presbyterian conscience. It's nagging me, but I can't ask for a new assignment as long as you have no American passport."

I said I failed to see what my having an American passport had to do with his re-assignment as a foreign correspondent.

"For one thing, it wouldn't be practical for me to be traveling on one sort of passport and you on another. It would complicate our lives more than they're already complicated. For another thing, some countries are a bit squeamish about admitting Soviet citizens."

"What's squeamish?"

"Reluctant—"

"If they don't want me then I don't want them."

"Logical but not practical."

"You mean we've got to leave America?" I asked.

"I'm afraid so, darling."

"But why?"

"Look, a long time ago I elected for foreign service. I've

been in it for fourteen years. I really don't know anyone
here any more. My contacts are all in foreign countries."

"Don't you like living and working in America?"

"Oh, yes, but I've lived and worked here a long time
too. I don't want to sound like a crusader, but I think there's
a lot to being a foreign correspondent in times such as
these."

Very simply he spelled it out for me, pointing out that
the position of the United States among the nations of the
world had never in history been as important as it is today,
and that Americans are interested in foreign countries and
foreign people and their problems.

"Their problems are all mixed up with America's problems," said Eddy.

Pointing out that thousands upon thousands of Americans
journey abroad every year, most of them to Europe, he said
they would hardly go to this trouble and expense if they
were not interested in foreign countries.

"When they're back home," he said, "I want to remind
them of the places and the peoples they've seen, and write
about the places, things, peoples that might interest them
the next time they go abroad."

He smiled.

"What are you laughing at?"

"I don't want to get too heavy about this, but with America's new role as world leader, we've got to know and
understand other people and other countries."

"But I don't know America yet."

"True. That's one of the penalties of being the wife of
a foreign correspondent. You're always living in somebody
else's country, usually renting somebody else's house and
sitting on somebody else's furniture and eating off their
plates, but you get used to it, and with the way transportation is improving we can come back to the United States
very frequently."

"Where'll we go?" I asked.

"London, I hope."

"What, with all that rain?"

"All that rain and Winston Churchill."

"What's Winston Churchill got to do with the rain in London?"

"Nothing, but that's about the only thing he doesn't have something to do with. But stop being so Russian."

"I am Russian."

"You won't be this time next month."

"What do you mean?"

"I received a letter this morning from the immigration people. They want you down in Mobile for a naturalization hearing."

"Will I pass?"

"Of course you will."

Unlike Britain and a few other nations, the United States does not automatically confer citizenship on a foreigner who marries one of its nationals. One has to study, pass an examination—or at least be questioned by an immigration officer—and then go before a judge. I cite all this because many Europeans, Middle Easterners and Asians do not seem to understand how the foreigner becomes an American.

Eddy was correct. I became an American citizen with unimagined ease. I still am not quite sure how it came to be, but with Nicholas McGowin, a distinguished Mobile attorney and a dear friend, looking on, I made it.

As I have emphasized, my life in the Soviet Union was not always easy. There had been that matter of Stalin's secret police and the open hostility toward me for marrying a foreigner, and an American one at that. At one time my inquisitors even suggested that I divorce my husband, saying that if I took that step all would be forgiven and I could return to dancing with the assurance that my children would be well cared for. This appalled me, and yet . . .

Someone has said that Russians make the world's worst émigrés; that no matter how lush their lives in a foreign land they still like to sit around the samovar and talk and dream about Mother Russia. Yes, Russia has a strong hold on her children no matter how cruelly she sometimes treats them. I am not quite sure of the reason for this, but whatever it is I am no exception. Yet, when I wed a foreigner my mother put me straight on where my loyalty should be, saying:

"Remember, marriage is forever. He is your husband. You go where he goes. You may be called upon to change your whole way of life. This is natural and you must make the adjustment, knowing that though it pains me to see you leave us—and I know full well I may never see you again— I say if you truly love this man, then go and make his way of life your way of life. If you can honestly do this, then, my dear, go and go with my blessing."

So, all of a sudden I became an American citizen in the Federal Court at Mobile.

"Now that you're an American," said my husband as we left the court, "what is the first thing you'd like to do?"

"I'd like a Martini," I told him.

He laughed. "You're catching on pretty quickly. All right, you shall have one."

He took me to Constantine's, a charming old restaurant, and I had not one but two.

"Now, as a new citizen what is the first thing you want to say?" asked Eddy.

"I think George Washington was a bum," said I.

He looked at me aghast and before he could say anything I told him, "Honey, of course you know I don't mean that, but you don't know what it feels like to be able to say such a thing and know that no policeman, secret or otherwise, is going to arrest me."

During the long reign of Joseph Stalin such a remark about him by any Soviet citizen could have meant real trouble. I know of people who have been sent to prison for less.

I hope George Washington will forgive me, but I could not resist saying what I did.

I held my naturalization certificate in my hand. I was a Soviet citizen no longer, but I was still a Russian.

13 While we were living in Moscow my husband bought a farm. It was not a Russian farm, but an Alabama farm, some seven thousand miles from our apartment-house home on Ulitsa Narodnaya, a diplomatic-journalistic ghetto overlooking the Moskva River and not far from the Kremlin.

When I asked him why he did this he told me, "First of all, it's good business. In an inflationary world, land is always a sound investment. Then, to be perfectly frank—and this is probably the real reason—owning an American farm is an escape—"

"Escape? You want to escape, Honey?"

He smiled and explained that long years of living in Stalin's Russia, with the tapped telephones, the listening devices about him, a uniformed militiaman posted twenty-four hours a day at the front door (there was no back door), and plainclothes policemen following him wherever he went, these and other restrictions gave him a terrible feeling of frustration.

Everything he wrote for the outside world was censored. His travel was limited to a radius of twenty-five miles around Moscow, and that only along three major roads, with halts to stroll or picnic discouraged.

About life in Moscow in those days he has written:

"Living in Moscow for foreigners is like living on a storm-tossed raft. Around us is a sea of hostile people made more hostile by vicious propaganda. The secret police are the sharks around this frail craft and they have sharp teeth.

They are always slinking about out there in the dark waters waiting for some diplomat or newspaperman to slip off the raft. And when he does slip, they race in and rip him to pieces."

Even I could understand why he wanted to own a farm. He also subscribed to *Country Life*, that serene and tranquilizing magazine of elegant living in the British countryside. I could understand that too. Nothing could be more removed from the cold war than a farm in Alabama and the quiet articles in *Country Life*.

The farm was about eleven miles east of Selma along a paved highway and it consisted of five hundred acres of very pretty land. Large pine trees stood on part of it and the remainder was covered in what looked to me like thousands of Christmas trees.

One crisp, bright morning he asked me if I wanted to see "our" farm. I was enthusiastic.

Standing in a clearing at the top of a hill overlooking the flat corn and cotton lands for miles around, I asked, "Wouldn't this be a nice place to build a house?"

"Yes," said Eddy, "but do you think you'd like living so far from town?"

"I would like to live here," volunteered our then five-year-old Susanna. "I want to live here. May I have a horse as well as a house?"

"Yes, darling, if we ever build a house here."

Walking over the property with us was Green Suttles, one of my husband's old friends, a man who still lives with the childhood name of "Baby Green," sometimes shortened to "Baby," but more politely, if you can imagine it, "Mister Baby."

I have been hunting and picnicking with this slow-talking, gentlemanly individual many times and it always amazes and amuses me to hear him addressed by servants of the hunt and young men as "Mister Baby."

Mr. Baby told Eddy that he should plant the entire farm in pine trees.

"Greatest absentee ownership crop in the world. Look at those trees you planted four years ago. Look how high they are. Plant another hundred thousand or so and in fifteen years you can sell them."

I thought to myself that this must be the biggest Christmas tree country in the world.

"What'll he do with so many Christmas trees?" I asked. "There're not that many people in all Dallas County."

"These aren't Christmas trees, Honey," said Mr. Baby. "They're for making paper so your husband can fill them all up with words."

Then and now Mr. Baby is not the easiest man for me to understand. Having learned my English from a Southerner—who speaks Russian with an Alabama accent, by the way—I think I know the accent of the Deep South fairly well for a Russian, but Mr. Baby has the worst case of Southmouth I have ever heard. The above pronouncement on loblolly pines for pulp came out like this:

"Theynot Crismustreeshoney—they fo makin, er, pup pay-puh so yo husbin kin fillemupwid wudz."

"Do you really own all this?" I asked Eddy.

"I don't own it. We all own it—you, Vicki, Susanna, and I. Can't you ever get it into your head that what's mine is yours?"

I liked the idea but this concept of mutual ownership was unnatural for me, a person reared in a country where all the land belongs to the people, where the vast majority of people live in rented apartments and sections of houses, paying very low rents to the municipal authorities, and where private ownership is generally limited to one's furniture, clothes, and cooking utensils.

"You mean this land and all those trees are part mine?"

"Just as much yours as they are mine."

"Well, that's very noble of you."

"It's nothing of the sort. You're my wife. We're in life together, the two of us and the children."

A charming arrangement, thought I.

"And the car? That's part mine too?"

"Of course."

"Then why don't you let me drive it?"

"Because you don't know how."

"But I can learn."

"Don't be too sure."

My husband always had a theory that Slavs, particularly Russians, had no affinity for machinery. In my case he may have been right. I am still unable to drive a car, mend an electric fuse, or do the simplest mechanical chore around the house.

"But you can cook," said he in consolation.

Standing at the top of that hill in the southern sun, my feet planted on what I was assured was my own earth, was a tremendously satisfactory feeling. Deep down, every Russian is land hungry. This one is, most definitely. That is, as long as I don't have to plow it, plant it, and weed it.

"Wy ont yawl puta house on it na?" asked Mr. Baby.

"Eddy says we're going to England."

"Well, if yawl get tarred uh Anglund, yawl come on back hair, huh?"

"Sho will," said I.

"No horse?" asked little Susanna.

"England's full of horses," Eddy told her.

"Mister Baby," asked Susanna, "where's England?"

"Ova yondah, Honey," he said, pointing across the tops of the tallest pine trees. "Ova yondah long waze."

14 Although I felt I was rapidly learning English, I still had great difficulty speaking and writing it. That continues to be true. Russians are supposed to be outstanding linguists. Not this one.

My first real linguistic mix-up in the country which had graciously conferred citizenship on me came at church in Alabama. Going to worship with my husband shortly after our arrival we parked our car, the one we had brought from Moscow, and walked a half block to the large and stately red brick building with a lofty tower at the top of which was a big clock. I thought this very odd, a clock on a church, and said so.

"It's the First Presbyterian Church," explained Eddy. "You know, the Church of Scotland."

"No, I don't know. What did you say it's called?"

"The First Presbyterian Church."

"You mentioned something about Scotland."

"It's really the Church of Scotland, but outside Scotland it's known as the Presbyterian Church just as the Church of England outside England is the Episcopal Church."

"I don't see what Scotland and England have to do with churches in Alabama, especially with one that's got a clock on it."

"Forget it," he said, "I'll explain later."

"But just a minute. There's something I'd like to have explained right now. Why does this church have a clock on it?"

"As I was saying, it's really the Church of Scotland and

the Scots are practical people, so they put a clock on their church."

"But why a clock?"

"So people will know the time."

"But everyone in America owns a watch. I know they do. I've never seen an American without a watch on his or her arm."

"When this church was built everyone didn't have a watch."

"Thank you, Honey. Now I understand."

As I have explained, I called my husband Honey, although he claimed I called him Hoaney. Perhaps I did. Anyhow, I did not see any difference.

Inside the church, to my surprise, everyone was sitting down. In the Russian Orthodox Church the people stand. This church was packed. Only at Easter had I seen the churches in Moscow crowded. As we walked down the aisle between the benches these very well-dressed sitting-down people smiled and nodded.

"How pleasant," I thought.

My dear friend Alice made room beside her, her mother, and her husband, Charles. No sooner did we sit down than we stood up and a man at the front of the church, on a platform, a man who was dressed like a banker or a prosperous businessman said, "Let us pray."

As I was dropping to my knees my husband grabbed me.

"No, no," he whispered.

Very strangely, we all stood while the man who looked like a banker prayed.

"Who is he?" I whispered as we sat down again.

"The minister."

"Minister?" I thought. "This is getting odder by the minute, that is, if I'm understanding properly."

I waited for a few seconds and asked Alice, "Did you say Minister?"

"Yes."

"Minister of what?" I wondered, for ministers are people who work for governments, people such as prime ministers, and ministers of heavy industry. In the Soviet Union, Lazar Kaganovich had been a minister. So had V. M. Molotov. I kept turning this over in my mind. I remembered that in the foreign diplomatic corps in Moscow I had met diplomats who were ministers. At the American Embassy, Wally Barbour and Foy Kohler had been ministers and at the British Embassy Sir Paul Grey and Sir Jack Nicholls were ministers. So that is who this man must be—some kind of minister from an embassy. But what was he doing here in Alabama in a red brick church with a clock?

We prayed a few times more, never once kneeling, and we sang a great deal, but the songs did not sound like church songs to me. They were too lively, too singable. One of them was like a march. But I certainly was not prepared for what came next.

The minister began talking. He spoke very loudly and quickly and only occasionally could I make out a word. The man was very angry, too, and the more he talked the more angry he became. He was so angry that he got red in the face. He waved his arms about and occasionally banged a tall wooden stand before him with his fist. It was all very embarrassing and I kept asking myself why he was so angry with the people. They seemed such nice people. I knew a few of them sitting near us—Alice and Charles, Alston and Mary Minge Graham Keith, C. W. and Adeline Hooper, and Kenneth Harper and his wife. Our milk was delivered daily from Kenneth's farm and not only was the milk rich and creamy, but the Harpers were charming people. The minister pointed his finger at all of them. He seemed to be accusing them of something. I was almost afraid to look at their faces because the minister was truly giving them hell. At last, I could resist no longer. I just had to see how my friends were taking it. Squinting out of the corners of my eyes—for I did not want them to see me staring at them—I got another surprise. The people looked neither guilty nor resentful. Just the opposite. On their faces they had calm, sweet expressions. How very, very odd. Mercifully this did not go on much longer. With no warning, the minister dropped his voice, dropped his arms, and dropped his attack on the people, saying, "Let us pray."

While the minister was scolding the people—and I could hardly make out a thing he said—he kept repeating what seemed to be a girl's name, an Eliza somebody. It sounded like Eliza Bomination. Never in America had I heard of anyone named Eliza Bomination, but then Americans have strange names. Whoever this Eliza Bomination is, I thought, the minister is very angry with her. Even so, it seemed to me that he should not bring up a thing like this in church.

Something else strange happened too.

A group of men passed around large wooden plates. I thought they were distributing money to the people. Now I knew that Americans were rich, but I never dreamed I would ever see anyone publicly giving away money in church. This was too much.

Looking closer I saw that the people were dropping money into the plates, not taking it from them. Everyone did not do this, though. Some just put letters in the plates. Again, how odd.

As we were leaving the church I found the minister standing at the door, smiling and shaking hands with the very people he had, only a few minutes before, been shouting at. We reached him and he introduced himself. He was the very spirit of cordiality and he kindly asked us to have coffee with him.

At a large house next door to the church we met his wife—a dark-haired pretty woman with extremely white, even teeth. Several of the couples I had seen inside the church were here, but to my great surprise there was nothing but friendliness between them and the minister. He no longer seemed to be angry with them and they did not seem to resent the way he had shouted, pointed his finger at them, and pounded on the table with his fist.

I am writing this years after the event and as God is my witness I did not learn until after I got back to our automobile that this good man, the minister, had not been angry at all.

"That's Calvinism," explained Eddy. "The Church of Scotland is a God-fearing, dour church and its preachers sometimes get very excited about sin."

"But who is this Eliza he seemed to be so worked up about?"

"What did you say?"

"Eliza. He kept repeating Eliza. I thought he said her full name was Eliza Bomination."

My husband let out a whoop.

"Eliza Bomination?" he fairly shouted. "Why, he wasn't saying Eliza Bomination. He was saying, 'A lie is an abomination of . . .'"

And such was my first visit to an American church.

15 My honeymoon with America, my adopted country and the country that had adopted me, was coming to an end. Behind my husband was the writing of his first book, his first lecture tour, and his first prolonged residence in the United States in thirteen years.

Assigned by his New York headquarters to London, we were about to leave. The only thing lacking was an American passport for me. It seemed that we had to go to Washington and talk to that formidable passport chieftain, Mrs. Shipley.

At this period of my daughters' lives both had burning passions, one for television and the other for horses. Our Washington hotel provided no horse, which surprised and disappointed Susanna and me because we had become accustomed to just about everything being provided in America no matter where one went.

As for the TV, the hotel seemed to overdo itself. As we had two connecting rooms, there was a set in each room. This proved a paradise for Vicki, then eleven. By dashing from one room to another she felt she was missing nothing, as indeed she wasn't.

"Why do you love television so much?" I asked her. "You didn't seem to like it so much in Moscow and during the time we spent in Paris."

"I can understand American TV."

"How can you be so certain?"

"It doesn't fool me. I'm never disappointed."

"Why's that?"

"Because the nice man always wins, and he also always marries the pretty girl."

"Always?"

"Always, Mama, always."

"Now, why do you like American TV," I asked Susanna.

"I like it but I don't like it as much as Vicki, but I like it."

"Why?"

"Because of the horses."

"Horses?"

"That's right," said Susanna. "On American TV they have as many horses as they have people."

"And the horses don't talk, Mama," she went on. "And the men, they aren't nice to one another, but they are nice to the horses."

"I see. All right, both of you go on back to your TV."

Washington was wonderful. It was early spring and golden sunshine and blue skies were our daily diet. In addition, like Susanna's TV men who were so nice to the horses, Washingtonians were very nice to us. One of the nicest was Carl McCardle. I met him first in Moscow in 1947 when he came there as United Nations and diplomatic correspondent for the Philadelphia *Bulletin*. When General Eisenhower became President and John Foster Dulles his Secretary of State, Dulles brought Carl to Washington as an Assistant Secretary of State. That was his post when we arrived in Washington.

Here let me say that I was very fortunate in having a number of persons interest themselves in my case during those long years when I was awaiting an exit visa from the USSR. The list is long, but high on it were Ambassadors Charles E. Bohlen, Walter Bedell Smith, Averell Harriman, Generals John W. (Iron Mike) O'Daniel, Russell E. Randall, Admiral Leslie Stevens, Elliot Roosevelt, Faye Emerson, and Carl McCardle.

On that first Washington morning Carl asked us to come

to see him at his office. Our reunion was joyful and after we talked for a few minutes, Mr. Dulles entered the room. He and my husband seemed to know one another but it was my first meeting with a man of whom I had read and heard a great deal. To the Soviet press John Foster Dulles was no hero. For that matter, neither were his predecessors during and since World War II. *Pravda* and *Izvestia* and Moscow Radio regularly denounced them with equal force, but they seemed to employ some specially nasty adjectives in commenting on Mr. Dulles, who was, unquestionably, one of their favorite villains. Yet later I heard Mr. Nikita Khrushchev say of him in private:

"John Foster Dulles is no friend of mine. He is against everything that I am for and for everything that I'm against. But I'll say this for John Foster Dulles—he's an American, an American who *always* puts his country first."

Remembering Mr. Dulles from TV and newspaper photographs, I imagined him a rather terrifying man. I found him just the reverse, although he did seem to have very sharp teeth. During our conversation—the four of us sat at one side of a large table—I thanked him for his interest in my case. Talking to me very slowly, as if he were my grandfather, he asked if I liked the United States.

"Yes, sir, very much."

"But you're leaving it for England."

"I'm a wife. That's my husband. I go where he goes and he goes where The Associated Press tells him to go."

He laughed. "I quite understand. Carl and I too go where our company tells us to go."

As we were leaving Carl said, "There should be no delay in getting your passport, Tamara."

I was about to thank him when he added, "The Secretary has seen to that—personally."

As I walked out of the State Department I thought again how grateful I should be to Carl McCardle and to John

Foster Dulles, whom I shall always remember not only as a great American, but as a warm and compassionate man.

Thirty minutes later I was in possession for the first time of an American passport, a very precious document to me.

From Washington we went to New York, where I was to say farewell to my new country. But before we sailed on the *Liberté*, we had dinner with a man then very prominent in American affairs.

I suppose we must have been at least twelve people at dinner and during the meal our host said, "So, you're going to London on assignment?"

"Yes," said my husband. "I greatly look forward to it. London, in the early days of the Blitz, was my original foreign assignment. It's always a good story."

"Indeed it is," came back our host. "Now when you get there make sure to look up —— ——. He's the head of the CIA over there."

I saw my husband gulp in astonishment.

Back at the hotel I asked him what the CIA was. He told me, adding, "And no wonder it has trouble from time to time."

On the day we arrived in London, March 4, 1954, it was raining. As I write this today, thirteen years later, it is raining. Sometimes I think it has been raining for all those thirteen years. Nevertheless, England is a delightful land and London one of the world's most fascinating cities. By now I think I know London fairly well, yet whoever really knows London? It is so vast and so many-sided.

The British people do not realize it, but their weather is their salvation. If they did not have dreadful weather, most of the people in other parts of the world would move to England, and it is already crowded. However, the weather will not protect Britain forever from nearly suffocating overpopulation. As the people in its former colonies become affluent and with money to travel, Britain will be their playground.

People who grow up in sun-drenched lands grow to hate the sun and dread the heat. Eventually they will tire of being prisoners of their air-conditioning machines. They will escape from them, and with money to spend on vacations, what are they going to do? I can tell you. *All* of them will fly to Britain, that paradise of blessed dampness and heavenly cool skies. Away from their sun and humidity, they will revel in this charming land of gentle and almost perpetual rain where, instead of burning sands, treeless deserts, and fetid jungles with their snakes, crocodiles, and fierce animals, they will vacation amid green grass, a superabundance of flowers, and a tolerant and inventive people who will gladly show them unique ways of spending their money.

Year after year they will return to luxuriate in Britain's cool latitudes, or to follow the advice of their doctors, "You really must have a change of climate, old boy. Go to Britain and soak up some of that shade and rain."

16 Through John Waterfield, a friend at the Foreign Office, and now an ambassador, we rented as our first London home, a Queen Anne house at 22 Cheyne Row, smack next door to the onetime residence of Thomas Carlyle. The property of John Pilcher, now Her Britannic Majesty's Envoy in Japan, No. 22 is a narrow, four-story row house with as many floors, and eighty-four steps from bottom to top—I know, as I climbed and descended them several times every day and night.

We had what the British call "part central heating," in our case the central heating being limited to the front hall. The house was, however, rich in heating *systems*. We cooked with gas, warmed the bath water and the little hall with a coke-fired boiler, used electric heaters in the bedrooms and dining room, and coal-and-wood-fed open fireplaces in the drawing room and the library-music room. Gas, coke, coal, wood, and electricity. All we lacked was atomic energy.

Some earlier owner had sold off to the proprietors of the house next door—not Carlyle—most of what was once a long, walled garden. What was left was a tiny portion of dank ground on which in spring and summer the sun shone for less than an hour. In autumn and winter it ignored our mini-garden altogether. As is often the case on the European continent, the lavatories were separated from the bathrooms, and in these lavatories there was no heating device of any kind. We referred to the coldest of these as the white hell of Chelsea. The delightful Pilchers, as they moved off to represent the Queen in Madrid, briefed us on Chelsea and

London life generally, but not on how to cope with a sun-shunned garden and arctic bathrooms.

Mentioning a street only a block away, Mr. Pilcher said, "You'll have no reason ever to go there. Avoid it. It's neither interesting nor amusing; a very drab rum place."

How times have changed. Today it is very smart and at least one duke lives on that thoroughfare.

We dispatched Vicki and Susanna to a nearby private girls' school recommended by a fellow passenger on the *Liberté,* and by my second day in London I was happily settling in to what could be described with accuracy as my first-ever home. With the occupancy of 22 Cheyne Row, we inherited Angela and Gabriella, two Italians the Pilchers had imported from a diplomatic post in Rome. Angela cooked, Gabriella served, and together they cleaned. Their bedroom was at the top of the house, our daughters slept on the floor below, and my husband and I on the floor beneath our girls' bedroom.

One morning on our first week in London I walked out of the library to find a tall, robed priest standing in the hallway just inside the front door. Looking me over through a pair of thick-lensed glasses he demanded, "What are you doing here?"

I thought that this was just the question I should be asking him, but I meekly answered, "I'm afraid I live here." I was so taken aback that it was almost an apology on my part.

"Live here?" he said. "That's impossible. The Pilchers live here."

"They did live here. They've gone to Spain."

"Spain? Why to Spain?"

"Mr. Pilcher has gone there to be the British Minister."

"Well," said the priest, "he'd hardly go there to be the Spanish Minister, would he?"

I made no reply. How could I?

"What's your name?"

I told him.

"Gilmore? Gilmore's Scottish. You're not Scottish."

"I'm Russian."

"What, with a name like Gilmore? Impossible."

"Come, Father," I said, "let's go up to the drawing room and have some coffee."

"Thank you, I shall."

As I filled him with Angela's strong brew I explained our presence in the Pilchers' home. He listened patiently and then said, "Come to think of it, the Pilchers did explain they were going away, and I also believe they said you would be taking the house."

Pausing, he shook his head, saying to himself, "Very odd, very, very odd."

"What's odd, Father?"

"A Russian married to an American with a Scottish name who rented the Pilchers' house. Yes, very odd."

"What's your name, Father?"

"De Zulueta. My church is up the road at the corner of Upper Cheyne Row."

"We knew a Philip de Zulueta in Moscow—"

"Nephew. Thank you for the coffee. I must go." He studied me with gray eyes over his spectacles for several moments, turned and walked out of the house muttering to himself. In time we got to know him well and found him a delightful, though highly unusual man.

A couple of days after finding Father de Zulueta in the front hall I answered the doorbell and encountered a blond, hatless young man standing there.

"Good morning," he announced, with a nice smile, "I've come for my bath."

"Your what?"

"My bath." Under his arm I saw a rolled-up towel. "I always bath here."

"Well, I'm terribly sorry," I told him, "but my daughters are having a bath."

"I don't mind one bit. I'll wait inside."

I thought now was the time to be firm. "I don't know who you are or what arrangement you've had in the past," I began, "but this is my home, and I'm afraid . . . well, if you've been having baths here, you'd better find another place. We've taken the house for a long time."

"All right," he said, again smiling. "Toodleooo."

"Toodleooo," said I, returning to my housework and saying to myself, "I'm sure of one thing about England—it's different."

Life in London continued to be full of surprises and fascinating people—especially for a husband and wife who had been living under a sort of house arrest in Stalin's Russia. In a way this had isolated Eddy from the rest of the world, and he was very out-of-date on scores of the little things that make up a broad society. He rationalized his blank spots by saying that trying to report from the Soviet Union kept him too busy to keep abreast correctly of developments in other areas of the world, other than, of course, major news developments. During the short residence we had enjoyed in the United States we learned for one thing that we were unfamiliar with the western world's ever-changing cast of characters whose names, for one reason or another, make headlines. I do not mean the politicians and the diplomats, for my husband's profession brought him in contact with many of these. I refer to the in-vogue movie actors and actresses, painters, scientists, socialites, writers, criminals, artists, businessmen, educators, athletes, and so on. So, when a jazz friend of Eddy's asked us if we would like to meet Gregory Peck, I asked, "Who's he?" Anyhow, we met him and I discovered what a lot of other people have—a rare breed of actor. A good actor, of course, but one with a deep interest in affairs outside himself, the theater, and the film studios; an actor who will talk about himself only when he knows that he must do so to help in publicizing a new production. From the moment

I met Veronique, who was on the eve of becoming Mrs. Peck, I liked her too. For one thing, her mother is just as Russian as I am.

One day the same jazz friend who introduced us to the Pecks, Ernest Anderson, dropped into Cheyne Row and said, "Do you know who's coming to London?"

"Who?" asked I.

"Mike Todd." Ernie spoke his name as if he were referring to royalty or Louis Armstrong.

I looked blank and I am afraid Eddy did too.

"You mean you don't know Mike Todd?"

"I keep telling you, Ernie, that Tamara and I have been on ice in Siberia for the last twelve years. We've been out of touch."

Ernie looked hurt, as if by not knowing Mike Todd we had let him down, and ourselves too. "You're kidding. You mean you really don't know Mike Todd?"

"Oh, I've heard of him vaguely, but I certainly don't know him," Eddy insisted.

"Well"—and this with a sigh—"I'll tell you about Mike. Why, he's er, ah, fabulous, and I want you to know him."

This we did—after a long evening devoted almost exclusively to anecdotes and enthusiastic descriptions by Mr. Anderson.

Michael Todd possessed the bluest male eyes I have ever seen, and dancing about as they did, up and down and sideways, they were never still. In keeping with his restless eyes, he walked about in what for a short man were very long strides, his head lowered and a cigar protruding from the right-hand corner of his mouth, like a bowsprit on a sailing boat. He kept the cigar clamped between his teeth at no ordinary smoker's angle. I have noticed that most men who talk or walk or do both with cigars in their mouths, retain them at sharp angles to their faces, sometimes as much as forty-five degrees. Not so Mike Todd. The shape of his teeth must have had something to do with it, for this addendum from Havana—Mike was pre-Castro—always jutted forward, parallel with his nose.

We encountered him first in the Oliver Messel suite of London's Dorchester Hotel, where he was playing host to a number of show-business people, among whom were the late Sir Alexander Korda, the film producer, his gorgeous wife, Alexa, later to die so tragically, and Peter Ustinov. In a Russian aside my husband identified them to me.

"Ustinov?" I said to myself. "He must be Russian."

"Do you speak Russian?" I asked this bear of a man.

"Da, da," he replied, adding a few other simple words in Russian, and without a trace of an accent.

How pleasant it was to find that one of Mr. Todd's guests spoke my language so perfectly. Accordingly I set off in a full flight of Russian, with Mr. Ustinov nodding his huge curly head, lowering that long upper lip, and occasionally inserting a word of his own. I found him the perfect listener, and he seemed to be following my every word, fascinated, I thought, by my discourse. Finally he turned to Eddy and said in English, "I find your wife utterly charming, but I haven't understood a word she's said except 'Da.'"

"But, Mr. Ustinov," I said in English, "you speak perfect Russian."

Adopting my accent, he said, "Thenk yu. The few vorrds I know I perhaps pronounce perfactly, but I heff poor vokabulary. Eet is limited to da and nyet."

"What a fool he must think me," I said to myself.

Over the years we got to know Peter and his superphotogenic wife, Suzanne, exceedingly well. To me he is one of the world's most gifted men—superb actor, director, writer, painter, and an exceptional mimic. He possesses the most sensitive ear imaginable. His hearing sense is so accurate that as a child he would play a game—the automobile game—at which to the considerable annoyance of his little friends, he never failed to win.

With his playmates he would sit at the top of a hill in west London. At his instructions they would turn their backs to the bottom of the hill, so that they could not see the make of automobile chugging its way toward them. This was well before World War II and cars in those days did not roll about London in their present great numbers. The point of the game was to guess, from the *sound* of the motor, what make of automobile was approaching.

The former actress, Maria Brietneva, now Lady St. Just, who told me the story, remarked, "It was maddening because Petka was never, never wrong."

From the Dorchester, Mr. Todd took fourteen of us to dinner at the old Cafe de Paris where Noel Coward was starring. I did not know who Mr. Coward was, but I soon learned.

Peter was placed with his broad back to what served as the stage. My husband faced him, at the other end of a long table, which meant that the faces of Coward and Ustinov were directly in his line of vision.

"In a way," Eddy explained to me later, "it was the most wildly bewildering experience of my life."

Acting comes as naturally to Peter Ustinov as do breathing and eating, and acting is such a part of his makeup that he is always at it. I feel certain that this is through no desire to dominate a dinner table, a drawing room, or an outdoor picnic—and I have seen him at them, too. With no disrespect to Mr. Coward, Peter mugged his way through the Cafe de Paris' star act, squeezing and contorting his large, full face into a galvanizing impersonation of the man performing behind him, which must have been no easy thing.

"It was like watching a tennis game—vertically," said Eddy. "Instead of shifting right-left, left-right with every volley, my eyes went north-south, south-north as they followed both Coward and Ustinov."

Long after midnight our host took us home and came in for a final drink. So began two warm friendships; the one with Mike to end with such dreadful abruptness, but the one with Peter and Suzanne to blossom.

17 Never once during my husband's long residence in Russia did I ever accompany him on a newspaper story, yet here we were in London less than a month, and I had been out on, I suppose, a dozen stories, or parties and dinners connected with his work. I liked being the wife of a foreign correspondent, for I got to know many of the people that he knew and met. I did not have to go out on Mike Todd's story, though, for the story came to me—literally.

Looking for a locale to film the opening sequences of his *Around the World in Eighty Days*, Mike selected the very street in which we lived, Cheyne Row. I invited him to use our house, No. 22, as his location headquarters. Coming home from his office on the first day of this arrangement, I thought my husband would faint as he sighted the maze of trucks, cameras, technicians, actors and actresses, and the long coils of wire outside our house. But a greater surprise awaited him in our library. As Eddy entered he found Mike in lengthy transatlantic telephone conversation with someone in Los Angeles, or thereabouts.

"Hi," called out Mike, waving over his shoulder with his cigar. "This won't take a minute." He was right. It took about thirty-five minutes. "I've put the charges on your phone," he explained as he finally hung up. "It's easier this way. We'll sort it out later."

Like so many movie makers, Mike could not be in the same room with a telephone without using it. He could no more ignore a telephone instrument than a cat can a mouse. He was the most compulsive telephone user I have ever known.

After a few words of greeting and expressions of thanks for the use of our house—out of whose doors and windows now stretched electric cables and wires with the profusion of ivy on the stately homes of England—Mike sprang back to the telephone.

"I wanna speak to Tokyo," he said, giving a number. Tokyo? Why, that was in Japan!

As he gave our name and number, I watched Eddy's face sag. "I'm getting myself a drink," he said to me in Russian. "I need one."

For four days we had a very busy house. That great Mexican comedian, Cantinflas (Mario Moreno), used our drawing room as a dressing room, the electricians blew out several dozen fuses—but always replaced them—and Mr. Todd continued to make telephone calls all over the world. I cannot remember what the calls amounted to, but it was a staggering sum—more than our present busy telephone, with three extensions and daughters using them all the time, runs up in five years. Mike, of course, took care of all the bills, persuading Britain's General Post Office to render him a separate account.

In the midst of the filming of *Around the World* on our street, Major Robert McLean, publisher of the Philadelphia *Bulletin*, and then president of The Associated Press, arrived in London on a vacation with Mrs. McLean and to our house to lunch.

"With all these film people about, how will I ever do it?" I asked in despair, thinking of the discomfort our present set-up must cause our guests from Philadelphia.

"Oh," said my husband, "they're newspaper people. They're used to confusion."

They came, lunched, said they found it a lot of fun and took as an immediate liking to Mike Todd, as he did to them.

One morning, in the middle of the filming, I saw a familiar young man sauntering down Cheyne Row, stepping lightly over the cables and adroitly avoiding the paraphernalia of movie making. He seemed to be headed for the pub on the corner, the King's Head and Eight Bells. He was that unorthodox—which one isn't?—Irishman, Kevin O'Donovan McClory, whom we had met with Gregory Peck at Fishguard during John Huston's filming of *Moby Dick*.

Kevin stopped and as he and I were talking, Mike leaped out of the house. I introduced them and from that introduction on our front steps, a lot developed. Kevin was hired, then and there, to work as a technician on *Around the World*. Mike took such a liking to him that for the Far East sequences of the picture, he turned over a camera crew to Kevin and let him film on his own. Later, in California, it was Kevin who introduced Mike to Elizabeth Taylor, who, of course, became Mrs. Todd.

Mike made decisions almost with the speed with which he blinked those very blue eyes. One Friday afternoon around three o'clock he telephoned my husband and asked, "How'd you like to go to France?"

"I always like to go to France."

"What about Tamara?"

"She also likes to go to France."

"All right, if you like it so much be ready for a five-o'clock takeoff. I'll come by for you at four."

"Take off from where?"

"I'll look after that. You just be ready."

Fifteen minutes late, Mike and a chauffeur arrived for us. Miraculously, I was *almost* ready, a rare thing for me. We hurried to old Croydon Airport, now closed, and then only used for private planes. Mike, of course, had one.

As the plane raced down the runway to sail into the air, Mike jerked open a portable bar and commenced opening bottles. In the process of opening and pouring, he suddenly looked up, and for no reason that I can imagine asked above the roar of the motors, "Do you know my name?"

"Of course," said Eddy.

"All right, what is it?"

"Michael Todd."

"Wrong. It's Goldboggen. Goldboggen."

"So what?" asked my husband.

"Just thought you should know."

"This sounds like a confession."

"Naw."

That was all there was to it. Neither my husband nor I ever knew why Mike—with a bottle in one hand and a glass in the other as his plane roared down the runway—chose to tell us a fact of birth which could have no possible relation to anything that we could think of. There was nothing more, just that.

Over the Channel the pilot told us that the airport near Deauville, for which we were heading, was closing.

"Tell 'em to keep it open," said Mike, shouting down the length of his cigar.

"We can't do that, Mr. Todd."

"Who the hell says we can't. Tell 'em to keep it open."

The pilot spoke into his radio microphone.

"They won't do it, Mr. Todd."

"Tell 'em I'll pay 'em extra."

"It's just a small airport, Mr. Todd."

"All the more reason they oughta wanna make some more dough."

Back to his mike went the pilot.

"It's no use," he said, once more removing his earphones to talk to us.

"Why, what's the matter?"

"It's only a small airport."

"You've already made that point."

"Well, the fellow in charge says his wife's having a baby, and he's got to hurry to the hospital. I'm sorry, Mr. Todd."

"Just like a Frenchman," growled Mike. "You'd know it, wunnaya? Some damned dame."

I cannot remember at which airport we finally landed, but wherever it was, everyone seemed delighted to see Mike. I also recall that it was a long way from Deauville because the car which our host hired, with driver, took a long time to get there.

"Can you be ready in twenty minutes?" asked Mike as hours later we checked into the hotel.

"Oh, Mike," I pleaded, "give me a few extra minutes."

"Awl rite, sweetie." He laughed and gave what he supposed was an imitation of my accent, "Fife extra meenits."

With Mike a pace in front of us—as if he were running interference on hostile ground—we arrived at the casino.

"I'm gonna play chemmy," he announced. "You two make yourself at home."

"That man looks familiar," I said, nodding toward a thin, dark, dinner-jacketed individual.

"He should," said Mike. "His picture's in the papers enough." With that he introduced the late Porfirio Rubirosa.

"And the other man not only *looks* familiar, but *is,*" said my husband and called out, "Tolya."

A shortish man with a full head of blond hair turning gray came hurrying across our section of the casino, and he and my husband held a loud and happy reunion. It was Anatole Litvak, the Russian-born film director, and as it was quickly explained to me, the last time they had seen one another had been in a slit trench, by the light of exploding German bombs, on the broad plain outside Poltava in the Ukraine.

During the last days of the war, Stalin was persuaded by his western allies to participate in a complicated operation which would allow the American Air Force to fly a shuttle bombing operation over Germany, occupied Poland, and Rumania. Vital to this undertaking were three American bases in the Ukraine. They were fairly safe bases until one night, through no fault of the Americans, they came in for a terrible pounding from the Luftwaffe. As Stalin had insisted on the Soviets' providing the sole ground and air protection for the American bases, there was not much the Americans could do in the way of fighting back during the all-night-long raid. I have heard my husband say that the destruction of American planes on the ground at Poltava constituted the worst disaster of that type after Pearl Harbor. Because of Russian and American censorship, Eddy and other correspondents who witnessed the attack were never able to get a full story of the destruction to American newspapers. Anyhow, Anatole Litvak, then a naturalized American and a full colonel in the American Air Force on a special mission to the Soviet Union, met Eddy during that raid, and Deauville was their first meeting since.

"Do you particularly want to gamble?" asked Litvak. We told him that we were not gamblers, that there was always too much chance of losing.

"All right," he said, "let's go hear some Russian gypsy music."

Wishing Mike good luck at the tables, we went to a gaily decorated little restaurant nearby, where the membership of the small band seemed wholly Russian. It was a long, happy, and nostalgic evening and morning for me. Tolya— in Russia all Anatoles are Tolyas—and Eddy must have done some gross over-tipping, for as we left to rejoin Mike at the casino, the musicians followed us not only out of the restaurant, but also down the street in dawn's early light, serenading us all the way to our destination. The bass player even lugged along his cumbersome instrument, slapping away as he smilingly marched behind us. Russian musicians do not make such energetic exertions solely for the joy of playing "Dark Eyes." I repeat, someone must have handed them a whale of a tip.

18 The many-nationed conference in Geneva in 1954 split up French Indo-China into two Vietnams, but it was an occasion of reunion for us and many Moscow friends. Covering the conference, Eddy stayed in that spectacularly beautiful city beside the jewel-like Lake Leman from April until September. The children and I joined him in August at a cozy and comfortable house on the lake front near Mies. In addition to other amenities, the grounds included a private beach with a dramatic view of Mont Blanc. The close-up view of old friends was better, though. How nice it was to see Secretary Dulles, Carl McCardle, General Walter Bedell Smith—who had once rashly offered to smuggle my children and me out of Moscow aboard his private plane as he completed his tour of duty as United States Ambassador to the Soviet Union—Chip Bohlen, Tommy Thompson, Bob Blake, the former French Ambassador to Moscow, Mr. Louis Joxe, and many others.

In a way, it was not half-bad seeing the grim and formidable V. M. Molotov, who was leading the Soviet delegation at the conference. It was Mr. Molotov who, only a year before in Moscow, had been the Russian official delegate to inform Ambassador Bohlen that I was being granted my long-awaited exit visa. At Geneva, of course, I was meeting the Soviet Foreign Minister on the *Western* side of what is called the Iron Curtain, which was in my case a reassuring geographical factor.

Living in a magnificent penthouse atop Geneva's Hotel du Rhone, headquarters of the American delegation, were

Mrs. Jean Barry Pochna, her tall, dark, and handsome husband, John, an international lawyer, and Mrs. Pochna's pretty sister, Ann McCormick, now Mrs. Robert Carmichael of New York.

At one time or another that summer everyone in the world seemed to visit this corner of Switzerland, including the Ruler of Kuwait, surely one of the richest men anywhere. Through oil connections John Pochna had some sort of connection with the Ruler, whose tanned and wrinkled face reminded me of a very large and very old walnut. This venerable gentleman invited us to tea one afternoon and it was for me a strange but highly amusing affair. The Ruler staged his tea party in the spacious lobby of the Hotel des Bergues, surrounded by his chamberlain, aides, bodyguards, and servants. Outside, his magnificent Cadillac awaited, a chauffeur at the wheel, to whisk him to the French shore of the lake where he was, presumably, enjoying the refreshing and invigorating waters of Evian.

The Ruler spoke no word of English, but he seemed to enjoy enormously the tea and the company—especially Ann, who was seated beside him. Her long, lovely hair was the color of well-seasoned tobacco leaf, and the Ruler of Kuwait found this irresistible; so irresistible that from time to time he would hand his cup to a flunkey, then run his long, fingers through the gently looping strands that almost reached her shoulders. Every time this happened, which was often, Ann would flash her sister a half-helpless, half-imploring look. But Jean, whether from tact, or distractions from other directions, ignored her younger sister. While these acrobatic explorations by the Ruler's fingers were going on, Ann tried to make conversation with the desert millionaire. From what I could tell, the Ruler seemed so fascinated by Ann, her hair, and her remarks that he demanded of his chamberlain detailed interpretations in Arabic of her every remark. At what must have been at least the fifteenth fingering of her hair, Ann addressed herself to her sister, saying in a loud voice, "Jean!"

Pretending not to hear—and when I saw this I deduced, probably correctly, that the Ruler must be one of her husband's clients—Jean gaily chatted away with Eddy.

"Jean!" This time Miss McCormick's voice was stern, but Jean continued to disregard her sister's heart cry.

"Jean!"

"Yes, dear," she said, at last looking around.

"Dig what this creep's doing to my hair."

The Ruler flashed Ann a wide, gold-filled smile and demanded of the chamberlain that whatever Ann had just said be relayed at once.

I would question whether "Dig what this creep's doing to my hair" can be translated readily into Arabic, but whatever interpretation the official gave Ann's highly undiplomatic observation, his master was tremendously pleased. Sweeping his right arm to his heart, he delivered a guttural that we were told was highly complimentary.

The tea party fingered on, but when Ann looked as if she could stand no more, Jean stood up, thanked the Ruler for his gracious hospitality and said that we, alas, must be going. We then followed His Serene Highness, his chamberlain, aides, and bodyguards to the waiting lead Cadillac of a long convoy. Bowing, we bade him farewell, and with smiles suitable for the occasion, watched him nestle, like a great crested bustard, into the rear seat of his sumptuous limousine.

The motor whirled. The Ruler barked a command to his chamberlain, who quickly rolled down the window, and from the air-conditioned interior said to Ann, "The Ruler commands me to request of you that you give him some personal expression of this, er—how shall I say?—leave-taking."

With a smile fixed on her pretty face, she said very sweetly, "Tell him to write when he gets work."

"Repeat, please?"

Ann repeated, but this time with more feeling.

The chamberlain said something to his master. Whatever this may have been, the Ruler's broad smile reflected his delight, and as his jet-age camel sped him away, he flipped a red rosebud at the feet of the American girl.

Recalling this incident of the Cadillac-borne dignitary from the desert, I should underline that at the Geneva Conference, Meester Gilmore had no mean transport system either.

Self-exiled in the city beside the lake was an Egyptian Pasha, an ex-senator in one of King Farouk's governments. He was a wealthy man, and one of his movable assets was a large and shining Rolls-Royce with an Italian chauffeur named Hector.

"Please, Mr. Gilmore," begged the Pasha one night. "I am soon having to make a trip of several weeks to Paris and London. Would you possibly help me by keeping Hector occupied? He is a nice, very nice fellow, but a very lazy one, and unless he is kept busy, he will"—the Pasha raised his large hands and arched his fleshy shoulders—"well, you know. Sir, please take over my car and occupy Hector's time."

"But, Senator, I have my own car here. I drove it down from London."

"Of course, you did, my boy. Just do me this one favor?"

For three glorious weeks we had at our whim not only a uniformed chauffeur, but also a custom-made Rolls.

Now I like jazz, but I like ballet better. With my American husband it was the other way round, so one evening when a ballet was being performed in one part of Geneva and Sidney Bechet and his band were playing in another, Eddy and I went our separate ways, I to the ballet, he to the jazz.

Back in the dim past, before my husband ever thought of Russia, he and Eddie Condon were walking one afternoon along a New York street near Rockefeller Plaza. To their surprise they saw Sidney Bechet sitting behind the wheel of a parked Cadillac convertible.

"My God, Besh," said Mr. Condon, "where did you get that Cadillac?"

Slightly irritated at this inference of his unfamiliarity with Cadillacs, Sidney looked up and replied, "Why, I wouldn't ride in nothin' else."

With that happening in mind and Bechet in Geneva, my Eddy planned his evening with care. Asking Ann McCormick to accompany him, he persuaded her to wear her finest furs and best jewelry.

"Why?" she asked.

"Just do me a favor," he told her. "It may not work out and I'll feel a fool if it doesn't, but I'd appreciate your help. The furs and jewelry, if you don't mind."

She looked exceptionally beautiful that night and the Pasha's Hector-driven limousine served as a complimentary vehicle to bear her to the concert of Dixieland music.

Eddy's seats were virtually on the stage, and of course Sidney recognized him. Between numbers this master of the soprano saxophone called out, "See me in my room after the concert."

"I have a better plan," my husband confided to the beautiful blonde beside him.

At the end of the performance, he sent a note back to Sidney suggesting that when the musician's admirers had finally left him in peace, he join Eddy at the stage door.

As a guarantee of the plan's perfection, Hector was stationed inside the stage door. Eddy and Ann waited in the car. The crowd cleared reasonably early and Sidney was not long in emerging. With Hector at his elbow, he was guided to the Pasha's car, whereupon the chauffeur opened the door, revealing Eddy and his lovely companion.

"Eddy," gasped Sidney, "where'd you ever get this Rolls-Royce?"

"Sidney," he said, "I wouldn't ride in nothin' else."

On General Smith's last day in Geneva my husband called by the Hotel du Rhone to say goodbye. The conference was over, the last communique had been flashed to the world, peace was to come temporarily to the Far East, and Smith, Undersecretary in the State Department, was flying back to Washington in Secretary Dulles' plane.

"How far up the lake do you live?" asked General Smith. "I can't leave here without saying goodbye to your Vicki."

"Oh, about a half hour by car," said Eddy.

Smith consulted his watch and said, "All right, I've got time to see her."

I should point out that when the General was Ambassador in Moscow, Vicki was one of his favorites.

"But, General Smith," interrupted a secretary, "you can't possibly leave now."

General Eisenhower's wartime Chief of Staff never easily accepted restrictions on what he could or could not do.

"Who says I can't?" he asked.

"In twelve minutes from now you have an appointment with Mr. Krishna Menon."

"Well, let him wait," said Beetle Smith—and I shall always treasure the memory of the man for this if nothing else—"Mr. Menon will understand. A child wouldn't."

Off he went to call on our then ten-year-old daughter.

19 Back in London we saw a great deal of Sir William and Lady Walton, and neither seemed to have changed in the slightest since our mutual voyage on the old *Île de France*. They were in the happy possession of two homes, a summer house in London and a winter abode on Ischia. At their London house we were introduced to a large number of highly interesting people, Lord Harewood, the Queen's first cousin, Sir Kenneth Clark, that icy authority on art, Sir Malcolm Sargent, the conductor, Yehudi Menuhin, Christopher Hassall, the late biographer of Rupert Brooke, and my beloved Sir Gerald Kelly, past President of Britain's august Royal Academy of Art.

At that particular time, Sir Gerald was cresting a high wave of popularity, for in his efforts to popularize painting and encourage people to visit London's many art galleries in larger numbers, he was doing a series of television shows for the British Broadcasting Corporation.

A small, greatly articulate, unpredictable man with a thick halo of fuzzy white hair, which makes him look like a Protestant David Ben-Gurion, he is one of London's rapidly disappearing real eccentrics. On one of his programs, as the BBC cameras followed him on a chatty tour of a favorite gallery, he halted before the little-known work of a little-known painter and praised the picture with rare enthusiasm.

"But was he a *good* painter?" asked the man from the BBC, assigned to keep Sir Gerald talking, which must have been one of the world's most superfluous jobs.

"Good?" came back the President of the Royal Academy. "Why he was bloody marvelous!"

A large part of the British nation was watching the program, and a monumental gasp swept across the United Kingdom, for never before had the word bloody been employed as an expletive on British television. It created an enormous sensation and, strange though this may seem, won thousands of new converts to fine art. People who had never ventured near a gallery decided to go and see for themselves something the President of the Royal Academy had described in such enthusiastic but shocking language. Today, when almost everything—including a full range of shocking four-letter words—is spoken on British TV, Sir Gerald's bloody seems awfully tame. But he made headlines when he used it.

He was seventy-five the evening I made his acquaintance, and I found him exceedingly attractive. Now eighty-eight, he remains witty, a splendid talker, full of charm, and the only man of that age I know who has, if he will forgive me for saying so, sex appeal. A product of Eton and the son of a churchman, he speaks beautiful English. Perhaps this is why, with my meager grasp of the language, I found no difficulty in communicating with him. Lady Kelly is as delightful as her distinguished husband, and we began seeing one another regularly, as we still do.

"I want to paint you," Sir Gerald told me as I sat beside him at the Waltons' dinner.

"Paint me?" I asked in surprise, for I had not the faintest idea who he was. "What color?"

"In several colors," he replied without even so much as a blink.

"Do the English always paint people?" I inquired.

"I do when I find them interesting."

"You mean you find me interesting?"

"No," replied Sir Gerald with a frankness I have learned

to recognize as an integral part of his makeup, "but I find your face interesting."

Only then did it dawn on me that he probably wanted to do my portrait. For a number of reasons he was a long time getting started and even longer in finishing it, but paint me he did, and during the Royal Academy's Summer Exhibition of 1966, the portrait hung there with several hundred others, a remarkable artistic and physical achievement, I think, for a man then in his late eighties.

Having dinner with the Kellys one evening, Eddy and Sir Gerald got to talking about W. Somerset Maugham, one of the painter's oldest friends.

"Do you know him?" asked Sir Gerald.

"I'm afraid I don't."

"Then the next time he comes to London you must meet him."

"That would give us great pleasure."

In this I enthusiastically agreed. I learned to read English before I could speak it, and the first English writer I learned to appreciate was Mr. Maugham.

The Kellys' dinner for the writer, his secretary-companion, Alan Searle, and us was an intimate but black-tie affair. As usual I was late and the party had already assembled when we arrived.

We were introduced, and Eddy was so carried away that he blurted out something to the effect that Mr. Maugham was one of his great heroes. At this, Sir Gerald led my husband to a side table and whispered, "It's my fault. I should have told you that Willy can't stand praise. For God's sake, no more hero worship."

"Then I've made an awful boob," I heard Eddy say.

"So you have, but I see no reason why it should spoil either Willy's dinner or yours."

It spoiled no one's dinner.

If Mr. Maugham had been irked at Eddy's enthusiasm,

he did not show it. He was gracious, polite, and wonderfully cynical about life.

He asked my husband his opinion about something or other, and Eddy prefaced his reply with, "As an humble journalist . . ."

Mr. Maugham, who looked to me like a very old and very wise turtle, lifted one wrinkled eyelid and observed, "Is there such a thing?"

I was enthralled as Gerald and Mr. Maugham discussed personalities and events of the past with an outrageousness that spiced their every give and take. At that particular time Randolph Churchill, Sir Winston's gifted, fearless, but often brutally frank son, had written something or said something on TV that was the current hot subject of newspaper comment and dinner table talk.

"He's only behaving as his father behaved at the same age," said Mr. Maugham. "Winston's behavior broke up many a dinner party when he was Randolph's age. The trouble is, nobody's old enough to remember about such things except Gerald and me."

In recalling his remarks I have sought to smooth out the way he talked. He was afflicted with such a pronounced stammer that what he next said, and the way he said it went like this:

"Like h, h, h, h, his f, f, f, f, father, Randolph is brilliant, b, b, b, b, but like Wuw, Wuw, Wuw, Winston, he can be b, b, b, b, bloody bbbbumptious."

Although his stammer was about as bad as they come, I found him as interesting to listen to as I did him to read, which is saying a lot.

London was very gay that spring of 1956, but hardly as gay as Monte Carlo where Eddy went to cover what must remain Europe's most publicized wedding for decades, the wedding of Grace Kelly to Prince Rainier of Monaco.

By the time the bells actually chimed, more than twelve hundred reporters, photographers, television, radio, and magazine representatives had arrived to report the event. When I saw what was going on, I felt sorry for everyone concerned. True, the Monégasques reaped a rich harvest of money, but life became almost unbearable for Miss Kelly and her Prince. They were followed everywhere, and at one point a Continental photographer—miffed at not getting the picture he wanted—actually lay down across a narrow road over which the Prince was driving his car, and then arrogantly dared His Serene Highness to touch him. At the same time, one could not help but feel sorry for the reporters and others assigned to this event. As is so often the case, they were but trying to do a good job for the editors who had sent them there, and in the fierce competition of today's journalism, the editors too were but carrying out their duties in trying to provide their readers with a colorful and intimate account of the wedding of two very glamorous young people.

Being alongside my husband, as I have on so many big stories, I have seen unfortunate and almost unavoidable situations develop between the press and the principals. If the persons who are making the news allow the correspondents and cameramen too much freedom, the principals are almost certain to come in for criticism. By going out of their way to assist reporters and cameramen, they are often unfairly accused of seeking publicity, sometimes by the very people they are helping. If the principals go along as if the journalists are not even on the scene, ignoring them, granting no facilities whatsoever, anger mounts, and they are called all sorts of names.

I confess that I really know nothing about such things, but at times I have felt that the communications of the western world are too perfect and too instantaneous. I feel very strongly that the marriage of two human beings does not demand hour-by-hour coverage by twelve hundred other human beings.

Among the first people we got to know in Monte Carlo

were a pair of the most amusing people I have ever known anywhere, Mr. and Mrs. Gerald Hale. American and very rich, Mrs. Hale was a lover and a benefactor of, among other things, cats. Her husband was an artist and a rather unusual one.

At dinner with them at the sumptuous Hotel de Paris, Mrs. Hale said, "I've just bought some land in Monaco, and I've told the Prince that I will build a home on it for stray cats, but only on one condition."

"What is that, dear?" asked her husband.

"That he will put an end to that horrible practice of allowing live pigeons to be shot from his casino."

"But, will he agree to this, dear?"

"He has promised me that he will."

"Then you plan to build the home?"

"Yes, I certainly do."

"And what will you call it, Mrs. Hale?" asked Eddy.

Before she could answer, Mr. Hale gleefully volunteered, "Why, Hale's cat house. What else?"

I do not know if Mrs. Hale and the Prince ever reached agreement, but I hope they did, for everyone, I feel, should like cats, pigeons, the Prince, and the Hales.

At this time I believe the Hales must have been in their eighties, or close to it, and they had wit and charm. I have discovered in this world that great wealth does not necessarily bestow either.

"Gerald has just finished a remarkable picture," announced Mrs. Hale one day at lunch.

"Thank you, my dear," said her husband.

"It's a painting of the night sky over Monaco," Mrs. Hale continued. "Gerald was very sweet. He placed it on my dressing table while it was still wet so I could be the very first to see it."

She paused, took another nibble at her caviar spread on wafer-thin toast, and went on, "Gerald said to me, 'Don't you like it, dear?' and I said to him, 'I like it very much, but as fine a painter as you are, I'm afraid the brilliance of the stars over Monte Carlo has evaded you, dear. I am not finding fault, dear Gerald, only stating a fact.'"

Turning to Eddy she said, "I don't know what it is, but the stars down here are brighter than in any other place in the world, and I wanted so much for Gerald to capture that brilliance."

"Did he, Mrs. Hale?" asked my husband.

"Indeed I did," spoke up Mr. Hale.

"Yes, Gerald, tell them how clever you were."

"Well—" he began, "but I think it would be more seemly if you told the story, dear."

"All right. You see, Mr. and Mrs. Gilmore, I had some loose diamonds in a drawer of my dressing table. For the life of me I can't remember where they came from. Perhaps a broken brooch, or that old tiara. But this is beside the point. You see, when Gerald agreed with my suggestion that his stars were not bright enough, the clever boy asked me if he could use the loose diamonds. 'Of course, you can,' I told him, so he stuck them on the wet painting, and you simply must see how Gerald's stars now sparkle in Monte Carlo's dark velvet skies. I tell you, Mr. and Mrs. Gilmore— may I call you Tamara and Eddy?—who but my clever husband would ever have thought to put diamonds to such a useful purpose?"

In that week before the wedding our friends introduced us to a great many people, and three of them especially stand out as I think back. They were King Peter of Yugoslavia, his Queen Alexandra, and the still glorious Miss Gloria Swanson, the actress. Being presented to a sovereign, however unruling, was a unique experience for me, a person born under a Communist regime, the very antithesis of monarchy and its royal trappings. I was a child of a system that had swept aside all titles of an ancient nobility, slaughtered an emperor, his wife and children, and in its haste to make all men equal, created a new aristocracy, and in

Joseph Stalin, a ruler more absolute than the last tsars. I
am sure that meeting a person who, only a few years earlier,
had been a citizen of the Soviet Union, was something of
a rarity for King Peter.

On being presented to him I did not know quite what
to do, so I did what I always try to do under unusual circumstances—act naturally. From somewhere I remembered
that with royalty one can discuss almost any subject, but
only after royalty introduces it. At least I went on that
theory.

Eddy and I met the King and Queen in exile through
the kindness of John and Jean Pochna, our friends from
Geneva, who now lived in Villefranche hard by Monte
Carlo. Working with a team of reporters from Mr. William
Randolph Hearst's International News Service was Mrs.
Pochna's sister Ann; so, in a way, we had but moved the
show from the banks of Lake Leman to the shores of the
Mediterranean.

We assembled at the Pochnas' mountainside house, the
Villa Iris, which commands wide and glorious views over
the sea and the crouching Alpes-Maritimes. Happily the time
was sundown. Since then I have watched the sun slide down
the sky in many lands, but nothing has ever quite matched
this colorful explosion in the clouds beyond Villefranche.
The air was still and warm and heavy with the scent of
mimosa.

From the Villa Iris, where I was told Prince Philip spent
vacations as a child, our party of eight or so couples drove
to Monte Carlo along the Corniche, built by Napoleon I,
to a Gala staged as only Monte Carlo seems to be able to
stage them.

During the dancing that followed a most pleasant dinner,
someone—perhaps it was Jean Pochna—beckoned me to join
her at the other end of the table. I must have hesitated,
for whoever it was called out, "Oh, come on, Tamara, kings
reign, they don't bite." I walked to the chair indicated beside

King Peter. For us both at first I am afraid it was heavy going conversationally, but as his manners are most gracious, he soon asked me if I would like to dance.

How pleasantly surprising, I thought. He did not ask me to dance. He asked me if I would *like* to dance.

Dancing did it. By the time the excellent band, imported from Paris, finished, His Majesty and I had started. By that I mean started communicating. In the spring of 1956 he was thirty-three. Soft-spoken and with black hair and eyes, he was an extremely attractive young man who also knew how to get around a crowded dance floor.

Conversationally, we progressed to the point that he commenced talking about his homeland, now ruled by Communists and, of course, one to which he is unable to return. But he seemed anxious to go back, understandably as King.

"While Tito's there?" I asked.

With a smile that was almost boyish, he said, "Perhaps he could be my foreign minister."

The euphoria of that entire evening—from the mimosa-scented sunset at Villefranche to watching the predawn sun light up the craggy Italian horizon to the east of Monte Carlo as we sipped champagne and ate wild strawberries—was of a sort that possessed a special magic for one born in a cold north country.

Off in a corner of the room the orchestra had slimmed down to a piano, guitar, and drums and I remember it was playing "La Vie en Rose."

Taking my hand my husband said with a sigh, for he too was a romantic, "Ah, yes, there's only one thing that this old country boy likes better than being exploited by millionaires."

"What could that be, Honey?"

"You," said he.

20 Returning to London we found it, as ever, brimming with Londoners and arriving tourists. Among the visitors was former President Harry S. Truman and Mrs. Truman.

Eddy had the pleasant assignment of reporting the day-by-day activities of Mr. Truman in England. Also working on the same story were Howard Handleman, of the then existing INS, and William Sexton, of the United Press.

London was at its prettiest and liveliest, for the time was late June, which meant the racing at Royal Ascot, followed by the All England tennis championships at Wimbledon.

Staying with us at Cheyne Row was Mary Hager, daughter of our dear American friends, Anne and William H. Hager, Jr., of Lancaster, Pennsylvania. Mary is a pretty, sweet, dark-haired, gentle young woman. Her father was almost as gentle, but he was violent on one special subject—Harry S. Truman.

One evening toward the end of the Trumans' leisurely visit, Eddy and our neighbor Peter Ustinov began talking about the former occupant of the White House.

"Peter," said Eddy, "I'm sure the Trumans would love your new play."

"Do you think they'd ever come?" asked the actor.

"I feel sure they would. That is, if they can ever find a free evening. I'll tell you what, you reserve a few seats for me and I'll—"

"Reserve nothing. If the Trumans will come to see *Romanoff and Juliet*, I'll give you the whole house. Well, almost."

This was no easy promise to keep, for Peter was enjoying a tremendous success with his comedy of American-Russian relations, built around the love affair of the daughter of the American Ambassador and the son of the Soviet Envoy set in some mythical country where Peter was the Prime Minister.

Fortunately, the Trumans did find an evening off, and Peter found the seats. Seated beside Mr. Truman, I had the unexpected pleasure of watching a man laugh until he cried. Several times during the farce—into which Peter was putting everything—the former President was forced to remove his glasses and wipe tears from his eyes. A marvelous sport, I thought, for he seemed to laugh loudest at barbed jibes directed at certain aspects of American foreign policy adopted by Mr. Truman's administration.

"What a man," thought I. "His sense of humor is not bound up by narrow nationalism. He is amused at the ridiculous, whether it be American or Russian ridiculousness."

As arranged beforehand, we took the Trumans backstage after the show to meet the Ustinovs, for Suzanne was there too. Peter and his wife had laid out a wonderful buffet supper, and he and Mr. Truman got along swimmingly.

Mary Hager, our house guest, was one of the party, and Eddy said, "Mr. President, I'd like you to meet an American girl whose father is a real rock-ribbed Republican, a Pennsylvania Republican."

Mr. Truman smiled. "I don't suppose he likes me very much, then."

"Mr. President," said my husband, "her father doesn't dislike you—he loathes you!"

I was horrified. How could anyone, much less my own husband, say a thing like that to this nice Mr. Truman?

To my utter surprise, Mr. Truman beamed broadly as he

shook hands with Mary, and said, "Come over here with me, Miss Hager. I'll fix that daddy of yours."

He motioned to one of the photographers backstage and asked, "Do me a favor, son. Take a nice little picture of this young lady and me. I want it for her daddy."

Later, Mr. Truman autographed the photograph beneath some witticism and, to my amazement, the next time we visited the Hager home in Pennsylvania, the picture was framed—and hanging on Mr. Hager's wall.

Bill Hager laughed. "As you see, old Harry got me."

I never cease to be taken aback at the give and take of American humor. Just how many Europeans, African, Middle Eastern, or Asiatic ex-chiefs of state would have reacted with such good humor as did Mr. Truman at having someone introduced to him as the daughter of a man who loathed him?

Yes, the Trumans are dears.

Another visiting American couple that I took an immediate liking to that summer in London were Mr. and Mrs. Casey Stengel.

One day about noon, Eddy telephoned me from the office and said, "Casey Stengel and his wife are in town. They're going to the theater tonight, but Case says he'll try to find time to have a drink with us at the house on his way."

"Who's Casey Stengel?" I asked.

"My God. I thought everybody in the world knew old Case."

"Well, I certainly don't."

"He's a marvelous man, manager of the New York Yankees—"

"Yankees? I thought you Southerners hated Yankees."

"Not Casey Stengel's kind of Yankees."

Mr. and Mrs. Stengel arrived at Cheyne Row at 5:30 P.M.

"Don't let us miss that curtain," said Mr. Stengel. "It goes up at seven, so we'd better leave here at six-thirty."

I am unable to remember just how Mr. Stengel, the manager of an American baseball team, happened to be in London. It must have been at the end of the season. Anyhow, I found the manager of the New York Yankees an amazing man—to say the least—but one whose conversation quite baffled me. Baffled, did I say? Why, I hardly understood a word he said.

"Don't worry," my husband assured me, "nobody else understands him either, but he's a great guy."

Like Mrs. Truman, I found Mrs. Stengel, or Edna, as she told me to call her, an extremely nice person.

Instead of leaving our house at 6:30 P.M., the Stengels to our delight remained until 1:30 A.M., staying for dinner, my husband and Casey talking baseball the entire time, and Mrs. Stengel patiently trying to explain to me what they were saying. It seemed a foreign language all its own. Mrs. Stengel tried mightily, but as I am unable to understand baseball, how could I possibly fathom Mr. Stengel, much less what he was saying.

Later, Eddy said to me, "Don't let it worry you. Casey's a unique human being, but the way he talks, well, that's something, and it's been baffling experts for years."

I am unable to remember which came first, the Stengels, the Suez crisis, or Italo. In any case, one morning I discovered that the population of our household had increased by one, for Gabriella, one of the servants, had been joined by Italo, a girlhood sweetheart back in Italy. As he spoke no word of English, Gabriella spoke for him.

"We want to get married," she announced, "and until we do, Italo asks if he may stay in one of the extra rooms on the same floor as Angela's and my room?"

"But I don't need three servants, Gabriella. I can hardly afford two."

"He doesn't want any money. He will look for a job somewhere near us, and until he finds one, he will be happy to help you and Mr. Gilmore."

"Well . . ." I said, hardly knowing what to answer.

"Having Italo will be very nice," said Gabriella.

"I'm sure it will, but what can he do?"

"He's a fine gardener. One of the best you ever saw."

"But you know we have no garden to speak of."

"Yes, I know." She brightened and added, "You can teach him how to be a butler. He can serve at the table. Señora, if Italo can't stay, then I can't either. He will cost you nothing, and he eats very little."

I told her I would have to consult my husband.

"He will like Italo," she assured me. "They can play chess together."

"But Mr. Gilmore doesn't play chess."

"Italo can teach him."

I telephoned Eddy at the office and told him the situation.

"Whew!" he gasped, "do you realize that the general manager of my company doesn't have three servants?"

"Yes, I know, but he won't cost anything, and if we don't keep him, I'm afraid Gabriella will go, and if Gabriella goes, Angela will probably go too."

"Do both of them want to marry Italo?"

"No, and don't be silly, please. This is a crisis."

"Oh, all right."

"He's a very light eater," was my parting remark on Italo. "And thank you, Honey, for having him."

Gabriella, Angela, and Italo were delighted with the decision, but I soon learned that there had been an immense improvement in Italo's appetite since Gabriella knew him as a boy.

He ate everything in sight, and not only constantly complained of being hungry but actually looked it. Aside from his ravenous appetite he settled down well at Cheyne Row. Being very religious, as were Gabriella and Angela, he found Father de Zulueta's Catholic church at the corner of the Row convenient as well as comforting.

Italo was not born to buttle. As a valet he was not bad,

but he seemed unable to get the hang of serving at table. I coached and coached, but he made small progress. When he had been with us for almost three weeks I summoned enough courage to give a dinner party. Among our guests were two of our first London friends, David and Virginia Ogilvy.

"Tell Italo that Lord Ogilvy likes new potatoes," I said to Gabriella. "Make certain that he gets plenty of them."

Italo smiled and said he understood.

At dinner, somewhat to my horror, I found him ignoring Lord Ogilvy but hovering over Lady Ogilvy, pressing the smoking potatoes upon her at very close range. Ginny took one or two. I was unaware that Italo had picked up any English at all but, nudging her sharply on her slim shoulder with his elbow, he said, "Comma ona Leddy, hava sum mo, hava sum mo!"

I had misjudged Italo. If he had made little progress as a butler, he was showing signs of becoming a linguist.

Italo was only a temporary addition to the household Gilmore, but another—and a more permanent one—was well on the way.

"A real all-American family," laughed Eddy one night a month before I was due to enter a nursing home. "Two children born in Moscow, and now the third in London."

"You wanted to be a foreign correspondent," I reminded him.

With two daughters, I especially wanted a boy. "And don't you, Honey?" I asked.

"A girl or a boy, it's all the same to me."

The night following his sweet assurance, we went with friends to a London night club, one we knew quite well. In the party were John Lloyd, The Associated Press's London Bureau Chief, his friend Joan, and Mr. and Mrs. B. H. Ridder, of St. Paul and Palm Beach. It was a club much in fashion in those days and, we assumed, fairly exclusive. Sitting around a large table in the center of the room, we were commenting on the general elegance of the ladies' gowns, when Mrs. Ridder said, "Yes, what a charming place and what lovely people there are here."

At that precise moment a fist fight broke out in a dark corner, where a youngish, blond man had been sitting with a lady of title who shall be nameless. The other man involved in the brawl was likewise young, blond, tall and broad-shouldered. As they swapped blows and epithets, they struggled toward us between the tables, upsetting a flaming chafing dish on their brawling way.

They reached our part of the room, but by then I had turned my back, as I make a practice of doing when some poor waiter crashes an armload of dishes in a restaurant, or someone starts a row over his bill. This proved unwise, for the next thing I knew I was knocked unceremoniously from my chair—accidentally of course—as the belligerents surged into me. I actually ended up beneath the table. My first concern was for my unborn baby, and as I groped about, I found something solid, the edge of the table I think, and began pulling myself to my feet. As I was rising, one of the young men, in trying to steady himself, stretched an arm out behind him. I presume he was trying to steady himself on a chair or something, but instead, his hand came into contact with my face, and down I went once more.

As I glanced up, absolutely terrified, I saw my husband's face. Never, never before had he so completely resembled an angry cherub.

"My wife!" I heard him say as he heaved himself from his chair and swung. It was some swing. It caught one of the battlers squarely on the chin, and that took all the fight out of him. In the meantime, Mr. Ridder, who must have been in his seventies at the time, grabbed the other young man by his long hair, and frog-marched him away from the table.

While this was taking place, someone helped me to my

feet. I knew the face. It was Jack Lemmon, and with him was Sharman Douglas, daughter of a former American Ambassador to Britain. Like us, they had been dining at the club.

Mr. Ridder and Eddy returned to the table, and seeing that I was all right, they looked at one another and smiled.

"Eddy," asked Mr. Ridder, "who were those young men?"

"I haven't the faintest idea."

"How old would you say they were?"

"Oh, thirty-five or so."

"And look at us."

"What do you mean?"

"Well, if at my age and your weight," said this American newspaper publisher, "we can clean up this floor as we did, then England's finished."

The next morning a headline in Lord Beaverbrook's *Daily Express* read:

WEST END'S BIGGEST NIGHTCLUB BARNEY IN YEARS

Fortunately our names were not mentioned.

21 My husband once said that discovering your first microphone in Moscow is like having your first baby. I am not so sure. For one thing, the newly found listening device neither cries, screams, nor bellows as do most Russian and American babies.

Russians and Americans, being great talkers and accustomed from birth to employing the full capacity of their lungs and vocal chords, both produce infants capable of making ceiling-shaking sounds. Geography *must* have something to do with it; you know, generations of living in those great open spaces that just beg to be yelled in. Carrying this theory to its logical conclusion, an infant of Russian *and* American parentage is the bawler supreme (ne plus ultra).

"But wait a moment," someone is sure to say. "What about Swiss children and Switzerland?"

True, the Swiss are excitable, and when involved in traffic mishaps, the world's greatest shouters. In fact, in every Swiss male there is a braying traffic cop fighting to get out.

The point is, Switzerland is small sideways, but up and down, Alps-wise, the Confederation Helvetic is enormous. Hence the yodel, and that noxious noise box, the cuckoo clock, and all those restless Swiss babies; again an example of the influence of geography on temperament.

Vicki and Susanna—my Moscow-born girls—must have established soniferous records in the maternity homes of the Soviet Union. Doctors and nurses were unanimous in predicting opera careers for each.

Born in the quiet backwater of London's Welbeck Street, my third child, Natasha, was different. She was not lacking in volume, but her shrill blasts were many decibels short of what her sisters had been capable. Without question, here was the incidence of geography operating once more.

Tiny England, where the inhabitants have huddled together for centuries, has few places where even a discreet hallo cannot be overheard by those for whom it was not intended. It is a land of subdued voices, where speaking loudly and with excessive force borders on vulgarity; where the raising of one's voice is a sure sign of emotion, the expressing of which just is not done, and where in an argument the first to say, "Don't raise your voice to me, sir!" wins half the argument right there.

So, Natasha became my English-born, quiet child.

What a difference in having a baby in Moscow and in London.

Vicki was born during some of the most desperate months of the war, when the majority of doctors and nurses were at the front, or in hospitals looking after battlefield casualties. Perhaps this is self-pity, but I still look upon Vicki's birth as an ordeal. I was simply directed to a large, unheated room—after a predawn race of four miles across the city in Ambassador Averell Harriman's borrowed Cadillac—containing several bare-board tables on which lay women writhing in various stages of childbirth. I was instructed to climb on a corner table, the only one vacant, where the nurse, who looked no older than fifteen, told me, in effect, to do my stuff and produce. It was only at the last minute or so that my doctor put in an appearance. He *was* in time, though, and I suppose that is what mattered, but a low point in my young life was lying in that chilly room, echoing with groans and screams, feeling terribly alone and forgotten.

Our second child, Susanna, entered this world on a January night during a Moscow blizzard. The war had been over for four years and nearly everything was better, yet there still was no privacy during one of woman's most private moments. As was the custom in Russia, I was not allowed to see my husband, or he to see his child, until the day I left for home.

In London's Welbeck Nursing Home, things were decidedly different, but two things were the same—my doctor showed up only a few moments before my baby, and again I had a girl. My room was a private one, however, with a telephone, radio, and television, and the sisters showered me with attention. I did not have Natasha on Britain's National Health Service, and from my few personal experiences with socialized medicine, that was just as well, for as a paying patient I was in a private nursing home with my own doctor.

As my dark-eyed little girl was born almost at the precise minute that a dear friend of ours from Moscow days, Admiral Leslie Stevens, was leaving it—victim of a heart attack on a private yacht—our third daughter was named Natasha, after my mother, and Leslie after Steve.

On a bright, spring day Natasha was christened in the Guards Chapel near Buckingham Palace, this being arranged by her Godfather, Colonel Roderick Napoleon Brinckman, baronet, late Grenadier Guards, with Ginny Ogilvy and Helene Stanley Smith, as she then was, Godmothers, and with our dear friend Jessica Lady Forres looking on and nodding her Scottish approval.

At last back home at Cheyne Row, Angela, Gabriella, Italo, and I—but I feel very strongly that it was mostly I—commenced marching up and down those stairs from basement kitchen to third-floor nursery.

"It's a beautiful, old house and we love Chelsea," said Eddy one day, "but those eighty-four steps are not for mothers with new babies. I think we'd better move."

Natasha was born on February 3, 1957, and in late March my husband was due for leave in the United States;

a glorious month or more in my beloved adopted homeland. We all went, Eddy, Vicki, Susanna, Natasha, and I. This was before the luxury of jet travel, and our westward flight was a little bit of hell.

Over the Atlantic, two hours out from Shannon, ice started forming on the wings of our four-propellered plane. We jettisoned fuel, turned back, and spent the rest of the night in Ireland. The following morning we took what was cheerfully described by the airline operators as the "warm, southern route," flying from Shannon to the Azores, then on to New York, a total of twenty-six hours with a baby of only a few weeks, but, I emphasize, a *quiet* baby.

From a combination of circumstances the birth of my child, the uncertainty of where we would live upon our return to London, and the discomfort of being on the plane so long, I was desperately tired when we reached Alabama. On that last leg of our journey, from New York to Atlanta and Montgomery, something again had gone wrong. I was so exhausted I wanted to do nothing but rest, a difficult thing among generous, hospitable people.

I am a great believer in the law of averages. It had been operating in my favor for a long time. As a Russian, with my fatalistic outlook, I knew all too well the averages were mounting against me, and that in my long stretch of good luck and uninterrupted happiness, the House Gods were being defied.

I was so right.

22 While we were vacationing in Alabama my husband received the following cablegram from Colonel Gerald (Oink) Smith, attached to the United States Third Air Force, stationed in England:

BEING TRANSFERRED TO AIR WAR COLLEGE IN ALABAMA STOP DO YOU AND TAMARA WANT TRANSFER TO OUR PENTHOUSE WHEN YOU RETURN TO LONDON?

"Remember those eighty-four steps," said Eddy. "Let's take it."

The penthouse to which we moved immediately upon our return to Britain commanded what must be the finest view in London. From its long plate-glass windows—which were more like walls—you could see for miles and miles in all directions. On a clear day you could make out objects as far as Oxford, more than forty miles to the north. Never anywhere—even from the Pochnas' penthouse in Geneva—had I ever seen such a view from the place where one lived.

Our penthouse was as modern as tomorrow, and I did not like it. I am unable to say precisely why. Perhaps it was because someone told me that a child had been electrocuted in what was almost our private elevator. Perhaps it was because someone else told me that a man was once discovered mysteriously dead, floating in the swimming pool. Perhaps it was because I am old-fashioned in many of my tastes, preferring old, gracious houses to the slick modernity of space-age architecture. Whatever it was, I did not like living in the clouds no matter how spectacular the panorama. We settled in, though, and I can remember making no complaints. I had been an American citizen for three and a half years, but I was still Russian enough to believe that a husband should make most of the decisions, and mine had decided to live in a penthouse.

We had been installed in our eyrie for several months when my husband flew to Holland to cover a state visit there by Queen Elizabeth II. Without him I felt desolate. I was incapable of explaining this to myself. As a foreign correspondent his work constantly called for travel, and we were often separated, yet, this time the separation was almost unbearable.

The second night of his absence I received a telephone call from a friend in New York.

"Brace yourself, Tamara," he began. "Mike Todd's been killed."

"Oh, no. Not Mike."

"Yes. In a plane crash."

That we would never again see this warm, fun-loving, dear man seemed utterly impossible. Devastated, I telephoned Eddy in Amsterdam and relayed the shocking news.

More was on the way.

Since the birth of Natasha, I had been constantly tired. No matter how much I slept and rested I felt exhausted, drained of strength. This was a rare complaint for me. What could it be? I was still a young woman in my late twenties. On my own, before Eddy went to the Netherlands, I had consulted a doctor. My regular physician was out of town, and a friend made an appointment for me with hers. He listened to me with some skepticism I thought, for he sent me to see a psychiatrist. I am not certain what this gentleman's judgment of me was, for he talked to me at length, drawing me out about my life in Russia, and then asked me to come back the following week. Both of these men were well known, and presumably eminent in their respected fields.

Dissatisfied and continuing to feel worn out and depressed, quite by chance one morning I dropped into a neighborhood clinic and told my story. The doctor suggested an X-ray and I had one on the spot. I was told to wait. Next I was asked to step into an office. The physician who had ordered the X-ray was sitting with two other doctors.

"Mrs. Gilmore," began a kindly-looking man with white hair. "I'm afraid I have some bad news for you. You have a spot on both lungs. The one on the left, however, does not seem to be as bad as the other."

"Spots on my lungs?" I asked. "What does this mean?"

"You must not be frightened. It means you have T.B."

"T.B.?" I asked in my ignorance. "What's that?"

"Tuberculosis."

Tuberculosis. My father had died from tuberculosis.

"It can be very contagious," he said. "Do you have a family?"

I told him.

"And the children's ages?"

I gave them to him.

"They must be brought here immediately for inoculation."

"But my husband's in Amsterdam."

"You shouldn't alarm him, but he should be told. I suggest that you tell him—now."

Poor Eddy. Again I telephoned him with bad news. We talked for a long time, and he was very sweet, saying he would leave at once for London.

"When does the state visit end?"

"Tomorrow."

"Then stay until the Queen leaves, Honey. Don't walk off the story."

"But I must."

"You must not. Anyhow, I'll know a lot more about my trouble tomorrow, for I'm being sent to see Sir Clement

Price Thomas. They tell me there's no better man on tuberculosis anywhere."

Eddy returned the following night and on Sir Clement's insistence, we made plans for my admission to a London hospital.

By this time Deolinda da Jesus da Costa da Silva, a handsome Portuguese woman, was living with us at the penthouse, working as a cook, maid, and nurse to little Natasha. I felt confident that I could leave my children and my husband in her capable care.

It was a dark, raw day when I said goodbye to the girls and Linda, and with Eddy set out by taxi for the hospital in London's Fulham Road, miles from where we lived.

Looking into the sad faces of my Vicki and Susanna, I almost broke down, and saying farewell to my little Natasha was almost unbearable. But, thank God, none of us wept.

Were we becoming British, hiding our emotions and keeping the stiff upper lip? Well, hardly.

The children, of course, knew nothing of how seriously ill I appeared to be, for which I was mercifully thankful. Mama was going away for a rest. Mama would be back soon. I am inclined to dramatize things, and I recall saying to myself, "Back soon? Will I ever be back?"

That is how desperate I felt.

The taxi started up and we rolled off in a gray, clammy mist, Eddy telling me one joke after another in a brave effort to keep up my spirits. We headed across Hampstead Heath, past The Spaniards, through Swiss Cottage, and approached Regent's Park. At the entrance the driver turned right, and up ahead I saw to my horror a motorized funeral procession going the same direction that we were going. With a gaiety so forced that it was somehow tragic, Eddy, I knew, was trying his best to divert my attention from the macabre business up ahead.

Surely, I thought, our driver will turn down a side road, for he knows where I am going, and for what reason—for he had heard the farewells—and I am sure he sees how ill I look. In circumstances such as mine, humans become ultra introspective, dwelling upon their own troubles and misfortunes, and assuming that everyone else knows about them and is sympathetic. Thinking about all this today, how could the taxi driver possibly know that I had tuberculosis and that there was some chance I might not leave alive the hospital to which he was taking me? On that frightful day I was not so logical.

Our taxi not only caught up with the last car in the funeral procession, but also, to my growing dismay, methodically overtook each automobile of mourners.

I believe that most women will agree with me that when one has been married to a man for a considerable time, and when the problems and difficulties along life's way have been solved and overcome together, one gets to know just what the other is thinking, and in the more sensitive of relationships, learns to know that the other one knows that you know he knows you know.

I shifted a nervous glance at my husband's face, and in a flash realized the mental agony that he was going through for me.

But wait. Our driver was to surpass himself. He next nosed his taxi alongside the hearse itself, just as it was coming to a slow halt before a red traffic light.

I was on the side closest to the hearse. Now in this world there are few less subtle objects than hearses. There it was—big, compelling, absolute, and unavoidable. It demanded that I look at it and its principal cargo, and I did just that. Inside the long, black limousine was the coffin. On it were the usual flowers, but at the head of the eternity box was a wreath of brilliant artificial flowers, and across them in bold gold letters on a black ribbon was:

MOM, GONE BUT NOT FORGOTTEN

As it has been said, between tragedy and high comedy there is but a thin dividing line, and this awkward tableau into which the unsuspecting cabby had involved us was high comedy indeed.

Turning to Eddy, I smiled and then erupted in natural— not hysterical—laughter. He understood me completely. He took my hand and joined in.

Taking advantage of the orange light before the green, our ever-eager driver swept forward, leaving the sad procession in our wake, and eliminating any question of our offending poor "Mom's" mourners.

This incident served as the relief valve. I got a grip on myself and began behaving sensibly, suppressing my self-pity and vowing that I would spend my time and thoughts on getting well and getting back to my children and husband.

Laughter is a potent medicine.

23 I am not going into the detailed discomfort of a major operation and nearly a year in hospital. People may be intensely interested in their own operations, but they will hardly be interested in mine—or yours.

I will just say two things about my hospitalization. It resulted in one of the eeriest experiences of my life, and the meeting of several persons who have become very dear to me.

After a month in London's Brompton Hospital, I was moved by ambulance some forty or fifty miles to the King Edward VII Sanatorium, located in the piny woods near Midhurst, Sussex, which is one of the most beautiful areas of England. My admission was to the surgery ward and my private room was on the second floor. It was bright, clean, spacious, and well heated. I had from my bed a lovely view of the flower gardens, the impeccable lawns, and a path that led westward into what appeared to be a dense forest.

As tuberculosis is contagious, my children were not allowed to visit me at Brompton Hospital. This meant that I had not set eyes on them for more than a month. On my first Sunday at the sanatorium, Eddy brought them down from London. Quite naturally they were barred from entering even so much as my wing of the sprawling building where I, and others, were awaiting our operations. How good it was to see the children. How sad it was, too.

As I was confined to my bed, my family lined up outside beside the flower beds on an elevated portion of the garden. Baby Natasha was too tiny to reach my eye level, so Eddy picked her up and held her on his shoulders. Oh, how I longed to hug them all. It was an ache and a pain all in itself, and one that was too much for me. I must be a terrible coward, for I could hardly breathe, and I do not think this was because of the condition of my lungs. It was the joy of seeing them again, and the shattering realization that I was so critically ill that I could not go home to them for months, if at all.

The sight of darling Natasha waving her tiny hand was what did it. I closed my eyes, and turned my head into my pillow.

How selfish some of us mortals are. Only after Eddy had spent a long time beside my bed, while Linda took the children on a walk through the wood, did I realize that seeing me under such circumstances must have had a demoralizing, to say the least, effect on my children and husband.

Later, when I knew they had reached the penthouse, I telephoned from my bed, and after saying good night to the children and thanking them for coming to see me, told my husband that as much as I missed Vicki, Susanna, and Natasha, and adored seeing them in the flesh, the experience was too heart-rending for me. "And for you all too," I added. "We'd better not repeat it right away."

There was a long pause.

"All right, darling. I think I understand."

The time was spring and dusk was late, and as I lay thinking one evening, a very strange thing happened. Ever so softly from somewhere I heard Russian voices. I looked about me. There was, of course, no one but me in the room. Straining to hear, I felt the owners of the voices were not in the corridor outside my door. But there they were, voices and unmistakably Russian; as if several persons were talking at the bottom of a well.

I do not know why I did it, but I turned off my bedside lamp, the room's only illumination, and lay in the dark listening. At the time it seemed that I might be able to hear better in the dark.

I found myself trying to open my ears wider.

Yes, I was right. Somewhere, somewhere, there were Russian voices near me. I tightened every muscle in my body and held my breath. Every so often I could make out a single word, but I was unable to fathom the sense of anything being said.

I felt perspiration rolling down my sides, my legs, my arms.

Yes, there were two Russian voices, one pitched slightly lower than the other. But where did they come from? What were their owners doing one thousand five hundred miles from Russia, in the depths of rural Sussex, and, indeed, if they were human voices, to whom did they belong, and why were they here?

Was I imagining things? Was I losing my sanity?

Raising myself to my elbows, I listened harder than ever. There was no doubt about it. My hospital room was filled with the muffled sound of spoken Russian.

Was it the secret police? Could they have followed me here? Stranger things had happened to émigrés from the Soviet Union. Leon Trotsky fled all the way to Mexico, but they found him.

I told myself that I was being ridiculous. Why in the name of God would the secret police of the USSR be seeking me in rural England?

Were the voices coming from the next room? No, this was impossible. They were too distinct to be penetrating walls. No, they were emerging from the darkness outside.

Again I lay still, tensing my muscles, holding my breath, to listen, listen, listen.

Unmistakably, those Russian voices were somewhere very close to me, and if they were not, then I most surely must be going mad.

Whichever way it was I was terror-stricken. In my fear

I switched on my light and scratched the wall, clawing for
the button that would summon help.

In came Sister Clements. Dear Clem.

I poured out my fears.

Standing beside my bed, she took my wet and trembling
hand. We said nothing. We listened. We stayed for some
time like this.

"I just don't hear anything, Tamara."

"Oh, Clem. There were Russian voices. There were. There
were. I heard them. I listened to them until I was certain.
Oh, Clem, you don't believe me, do you?"

She gave me a long look and replied, "Yes, I do believe
you. I'll see what this is all about."

"Clem?"

"Yes?"

"Could it be ghosts? Have any Russians ever died here?"

She laughed and patted my hand.

"No, dear. You're the only Russian we've ever had."

She left the room. I was alone again. Once more I
listened. I heard nothing now. Clem did not reappear for a
long time. Mercifully, neither did the voices. Then my door
at last opened and I saw Clem standing there. I asked,
"Have you found them?"

"Found what, dear Tamara?"

I sighed. I knew the mystery had not been solved.

So began a long, terrifying night. Despite rules I was
allowed to keep a dim light burning. The whole business
was about to drive me out of my mind, that is, if I were not
already out of it.

I lifted the telephone to call my husband in London.

"Do you know what time it is, madame?" asked the
operator on the sanatorium's switchboard.

"Yes, I'm afraid I do, but this is very urgent."

"Very well, madame. I hope we won't get into trouble—
you and I."

I heard Eddy on the other end of the line. Into the telephone I poured out my story.

"I tell you I heard Russian voices," I insisted.

I felt that he doubted me. How could he react otherwise?

He tried to reassure me by saying that perhaps I had left my radio on, that the BBC was broadcasting something in Russian, or that I had been tuned to one of Moscow Radio's shortwave Russian language services.

"No. It wasn't anything like that. I haven't listened to the radio all day."

"And the TV?"

"It's been off for hours."

"I'll have them check it tomorrow. TV's a funny thing. In certain kinds of weather, it can do freakish things."

"I tell you I heard real Russian voices, neither radio nor TV voices."

"All right, Tomka. If you say you heard them, then you heard them."

I got little sleep, but I heard the ghostly Slavic voices no more.

Next morning I found out all.

The explanation hinged on such a coincidence that it reads like something devised by a writer of bad fiction.

Scotland Yard was not called in to solve the mystery. No chaplain had to lay a ghost. Instead, someone on the administrative side of the sanatorium remembered that not too long before my admission, a Russian refugee, a man liberated by the British Army from a north German prison camp, had been hired at the King Edward VII as a baker. Questioning him after my experience, the management learned that the baker had an émigré friend working as a gardener in the Midhurst area. They often met at a nearby pub, but purely by chance, on this occasion, they had stopped beneath my window, in the dark of a spring evening, to have a chat.

The odds against two Russian-born, Russian-speaking

persons converging within ten yards of a third in the wilds of Sussex, England, must be very great indeed. But there it was.

And what a relief it was to learn that I was not being shadowed by the Soviet secret police, or losing my mind.

24 In the room next to mine, recovering from the ravages of the same disease that had ruptured my normal life, was a lovely, Yugoslav-born, young woman, Mrs. Inga Roberts. She too was mending—from major surgery necessary in the removal of affected lung tissue. As a friend, Inga was a joy, and as a companion a great therapeutic factor in my convalescence.

Under some sort of treatment in the room beyond Inga's was an Egyptian in his early twenties. We were unaware of the exact nature of his illness, but certain of one thing—his dislike of England, its sovereign, its government, political leaders, and its way of life. And he said so repeatedly in a rather loud voice.

On his walls he kept a large newspaper photograph of President Gamal Nasser, and another of Mr. Nikita Khrushchev. Since he was receiving medication, board, and private room at the expense of the British taxpayer, we thought him, to say the least, unusually callous and unappreciative.

One bright morning I had a rather special visitor, a wealthy Englishman, honorary private secretary to the Prime Minister, husband to a beautiful woman, owner of one of the nation's stateliest homes and a peer-to-be. While he was helping to add cheer to my day he heard the story of the ungrateful and arrogant Arab resident down the hall. One of the nurses was the informant.

"What's the number of his room?" he inquired.

The nurse told him.

"Forgive me for a moment, Tamara," he said as he un-wound his long legs, adjusted his spectacles, stood up and left me.

As I learned later from an eyewitness, he strolled down the corridor, stopped before the Egyptian's door, peered through the little glass panel, and rapped sharply on the door. Assured that he had attracted the undivided attention of the room's occupant, he stuck out his tongue, and blew Ali a loud and ripe raspberry, a Bronx cheer all right but one with an Oxford accent.

This is one of the native types I most admire in Britain—the undeviating eccentric who practices his eccentricity whether he be a pub-keeper or an aide to the premier.

The United Kingdom—meaning England, Scotland, Wales, and Northern Ireland—is the spiritual home of the real eccentric, who, though he lives in a world of constant change, remains a tough and rare old bird. Only a few months ago, Lord Arran, another splendid eccentric, related in London's *Evening News* how his father-in-law kept a lion cub with him in the trenches during World War I. Life in the mud of Flanders did not agree with this king of beasts. He became dull and listless, so the owner decided on medication, and to apply it himself.

"The last that was seen of the animal," said the Earl of Arran, "he was bounding toward the enemy trenches.

"Still, my father-in-law could proudly boast that he was the only man ever known to have given a lion an enema."

That was long ago, but eccentrics are still plentiful. When he was Governor-General of New Zealand, Lord Cobham claimed they are essential to society. He defined the true eccentric as one who pursues his own version of the truth and value of things, untainted by outside pressures or conventions. "He has a sort of crazy sanity," said His Lordship.

I know a man who keeps a stuffed camel in his home and has often been seen traveling on the London subway wearing

Japanese armor. And then there is the lady in Nottingham who runs The Fairy Investigation Society.

"People claim I'm eccentric," she once said in an interview, "but I don't think so."

This, of course, is the true test. Eccentrics must never think they are eccentrics.

My favorite eccentric—the one who gave a rude lip rattle to the unappreciative Egyptian—greatly helped me in my long recovery. But there were so many others.

Through Virginia Ogilvy, Mr. and Mrs. Herbert Agar and Mrs. Agar's delightful son, Billy Wallace, long-time escort of Princess Margaret, happily came into my life when I was at the King Edward VII Sanatorium.

An eminent American historian and former editor of the Louisville *Courier-Journal,* Herbert, with Barbie, live near Petworth, a few miles from Midhurst. To me the wise, wonderful, kind, and beautiful Barbie is, and always shall be, as she puts it, my "English Mum." In giving eternal thanks, could I say more than I am honored and proud?

I was very fortunate in having many visitors during my recuperation, and a frequent one was Kevin McClory from the John Huston-Mike Todd days.

He was at that time very much in love with a young, classically beautiful girl named Frederika (Bobo) Sigrist, of Nassau. During one of her trips to London, she was brought to see me by Kevin. We became and have remained the warmest friends. Bobo is now Mrs. McClory and I record with pleasure that I am the Godmother of one of their children.

Sir Clement Price Thomas, Sir Geoffrey Todd, head of the sanatorium, Sister Clem, and the whole staff of the King Edward VII were all that people said they would be. They cured me, and I am deeply grateful for the thousands of other things, big and little, they did for me. As they promised, I today lead a completely normal and healthy life.

In my recuperation, the good Lord and prayer were always with me. Despite his own illness and the frailty of great age, Father Georgi, of my own Russian Orthodox faith, came often from London to see me. As others saw to my medical needs, he took care of the spiritual.

25 The joy of at last being home with my loved ones was too obvious to relate here. But one thing was wrong—little Natasha did not know me. To her I was a complete stranger.

Since leaving her nearly a year earlier, not I, but Linda, her Portuguese nurse, had been her constant companion and substitute mother. On the subject of this good woman, I am unable to express the depth of my thanks. For twelve months she had refused to take a vacation, or even a week-end or a day off. To my husband's repeated suggestions that she must have some sort of rest, she stubbornly repeated, "As long as Madame's away, I shall stay here. When she comes back we'll talk about rest." Reminded that Vicki was now a teenager and capable of looking after her younger sisters, Linda would smile and say, "It's all right, sir. It's all right."

Born in Moscow, sharing the uncertainties of a home life inevitable with an American father and a Russian mother in Joseph Stalin's Soviet Union, Vicki and Susanna, long before my illness, learned to adapt to changes and sudden surprises. Had not their father been separated from them and me for nearly a year? That was 1951 when Eddy had been summoned to New York by his home office for consultations. He had to go alone, which was neither his desire nor mine, but the Moscow authorities refused to give me an exit visa. Then, when he tried to return to us and to his Moscow post, he was refused an entry visa. Vicki and Susanna were then old enough to sense my apprehension, as well as my heavyheartedness and real fears over the whole dreadful situation. To their credit, they behaved well and did not ask too many distressing questions about their father's enforced long absence. So, I suppose this must have had something to do with their easy adaptation to their long separation from their mother's hospitalization. I say they adapted without suffering any emotional wounds—I mean, I believe they did—yet, how does a parent really know about these things?

And my American husband, how had he fared with three half-Russian children and a Portuguese nurse-cook? He seemed in no way changed. Like Old Mr. Volga, he always just rolled along, but, as he insisted, "without the Volga sturgeons' fine, gray caviar and the boat song."

Long ago I said that my husband resembled a Russian general. He was big, bald, and barrel-chested, with a seventeen-and-a-half-inch collar. Since extracting his children and me from the USSR, his reportorial life had often brought him in close contact with highly placed Soviet officials, including Mr. Nikita Khrushchev. By the 1960s he had covered Mr. K's amazing—and I feel this is the word—activities in Yugoslavia, Switzerland, Britain, and France, and at the time of which I write, he was about to go off to Austria to bird-dog the Soviet leader on a state visit there.

"You know," said Eddy one night after I had settled down to my old life in the penthouse, "looking like a Russian general is one thing, but looking like Nikita Khrushchev is another, and I don't think he likes it any better than I do."

"You don't look like Mr. Khrushchev," I told him. "You've got a mustache."

"Not a very big one."

"But Mr. Khrushchev has no mustache at all. Anyhow, you're younger, taller, and you dress better."

"Not since he's got a western tailor."

"You've got a western tailor, and if he can't make you

look better than Mr. Khrushchev, you'd better change tailors."

"Perhaps I will. Then people will stop mistaking me for him."

"Do they really do that, Honey?"

"I can assure you they do."

"Please tell me about it."

He did.

"It began in Belgrade. I was standing at the airport taking notes on a speech Khrushchev was making. I was close to him, and next to me was the wife of a minister in Tito's Government. Out of the corner of my eye I thought I saw her paying undue attention to me. Finally she said very softly and in Russian, 'You may not like this, but you and Mr. Khrushchev look alike, very much alike.'

"Now what was I to say? She was the wife of a minister, and I but a visiting western correspondent. I gave her a weak smile, but her gratuitous comparison stung."

Eddy pulled at his pipe, blew some smoke out of the penthouse window, and went on: "Two nights later I was traveling along that long, straight highway between Belgrade and Zagreb, and my driver stopped at a filling station—"

"Did you find Khrushchev there?"

"No," he replied, "and please don't interrupt. This is serious. Freud could do a lot with it. Now, in Yugoslavia's filling stations I discovered that you can fill up with things other than gasoline, and one of them is Slivovitz."

"Sliv-o-what?"

"Your ignorance of alcoholic drink is appalling. Slivovitz is plum brandy, the national firewater of Yugoslavia. You're a Slav, you should know that."

"Well, I don't, but get back to that filling station. I've been in the hospital a long time. I need amusement."

"Well, I don't know if this is going to amuse you, but it amused me. I went inside the place with the driver to pay the bill, and I found I was in a bar. A bushy-haired, big man bowed to me with mock servility, screwed up his eyes, and said in Russian, 'Ah, so you're Khrushchev, are you? Well, welcome to our bar, Your Excellency.'"

Eddy said he told the man as emphatically as he could that he certainly was not Khrushchev, but the man—whose tank was full of Slivovitz—answered, "You can fool the Russians, but you can't fool me."

"What did you do?" I asked.

"I was deeply wounded," he said. "My feelings were hurt; so I did what seemed the best thing to do—I went out into the long Balkan night."

Eddy was silent for a moment.

"Then, after I got to Zagreb, it happened again. With some friends I visited what was described as an excellent Gypsy restaurant."

He thought the manager unduly polite and solicitous but put it down to Balkan courtesy. As the manager seated Eddy and his friends, he said, "Gospodin Khrushchev, our singer doesn't sing Russian very well, but she'll do the best she can."

A young woman from the band stood up and sang several songs in very bad Russian. "Her heart wasn't in it," was my husband's comment.

"That put you in your place," I told him. "What did you do?"

"My friends and I," he replied, "sent her up a bottle of very bad wine. But wait, I haven't finished. After we'd downed our meal, the manager came up again and said to me, 'You know, sir, back in the days when our two countries were warm friends, well, one night some of your soldiers came in here and they didn't behave like friends.'

"'What did they do?' I asked.

"'They broke up my furniture and glasses and plates,' the manager replied."

I asked Eddy how he dealt with this revelation.

"Revelation? It was more like an ultimatum. By this time I had gone so far I couldn't back down. I told the poor man, 'Now look here, you make out a bill, add twenty per cent for interest, send it to the Soviet Embassy in Belgrade, and just as sure as I'm Nikita Khrushchev, you'll get your money!'"

"You didn't dare do that."

"Didn't I? I tell you I did. I have witnesses."

"Well, what happened?"

"I have no idea, but I was doing my best to make a little mischief between those two Communist countries. God knows they've made enough for mine."

I still did not feel my husband looked all that much like Mr. Khrushchev, but the incidents of mistaken identity continued.

In Vienna, during the Khrushchev-President Kennedy confrontation, Eddy did one fourteen-hour stretch of reporting and writing and, after it was over and he was once more with a group of friends, went for a meal in one of those charming wine houses on the outskirts of the city. A member of a large and gay party at an adjoining table suddenly stood up and, pointing at my husband, shouted, "There's Mr. Khrushchev!"

Eddy smiled and waved, and then went back to the business at hand—consuming the large and much-needed meal. He was unable to finish though.

Several dozen diners commenced shouting in chorus, "Khrushchev, Khrushchev, give us a speech, Mr. Khrushchev!"

One never could say that to my husband unless one *did* want a speech.

Getting to his feet and, through German-speaking friends, who enthusiastically went along with the ridiculous charade by translating, he said to more than a hundred attentive listeners that while he was not Nikita Khrushchev, he was his brother, Dmitry Khrushchev, and was very happy to be in Vienna and among such charming people.

"But Mr. Khrushchev has no brother," said I, interrupting his account of the Vienna happening.

"Well, if he does," said Eddy, "I'm sure he's not Dmitry. Anyhow, I went on and, if I do say so, I didn't do too badly."

Being a gay, jovial people not given to taking themselves too seriously—was it not an eminent Viennese who once said, "The Austrian situation is desperate, but it's not serious"?—the large crowd in the open-air restaurant fell in with the mood of the Khrushchev spoof.

From somewhere nearby a short handsome man with graying hair produced a violin, and walking over to Eddy's table serenaded him with a moving rendition of "Dark Eyes."

My husband and the violinist sat down to resounding cheers.

"Do you know who that man is?" asked Erich Waha, the AP's bureau chief in Austria. "He plays first violin in the Vienna Symphony."

"Do you know who I am?" asked Eddy. "For at this moment, I'm not sure."

To the excruciating embarrassment of several persons, a report of "Mr. Dmitry Khrushchev's" remarks at a restaurant appeared in a Vienna newspaper the following morning.

26 "I feel so wonderful that I'm afraid," I announced one day at breakfast.

"Afraid of what?"

"Afraid that this can't keep up, Honey. You know, it's just like I'd never been to the hospital."

"It's precisely because you have been to the hospital that you are feeling the way you are, my darling. Or is it because you're going out for the first time?"

"I don't know. Everything seems so perfect."

"Even living in the penthouse?"

"I didn't say *that*."

It was going to be my first real night out and I did so much look forward to it. I was to see a ballet, and Margot Fonteyn would be dancing.

I spent the entire afternoon playing with Natasha and resting. I should put it that playing with Natasha *was* resting, the very best resting. It was on that afternoon that she called me "Mama" again, and I shall not dwell on just what this meant to me.

Life was normal. Life was good. Covent Garden appeared brighter than ever. Kevin and Bobo seemed gayer than ever, and Dame Margot Fonteyn was greater than ever.

Of all the ballerinas, actresses, singers, musicians—I could almost say of all the women I have ever met—Margot Fonteyn stands by herself as a person of great talent, immense charm, and that very rare quality of unlimited consideration for others. I have never known a person, unless it is my mother, who is more unselfish. For me there is a good Russian word to describe her. It is dushka, which means a real darling.

Our party went backstage to congratulate her on her performance, and to make certain that she was not too tired to join us for a late supper.

"Of course, I'm not." She smiled, and looking at her husband asked, "Am I, Tito?"

"Not if you say you're not," he said.

We supped at the River Club on a glassed-in terrace overlooking the Thames. It was a warm, early summer night and the food and wine were excellent.

In those days the River Club was presided over by Captain Leo Ponti, former French Foreign Legionnaire, ex-officer in General Charles de Gaulle's Free French Forces, and very much a man about town, and if man ever resembled a rooster, it is Leo, but a very special rooster with particularly brilliant plumage. The chests of all the pouter pigeons in the world appear to have been modeled after Leo's. With his chest thrust forward he marches about taking quick, confident steps, his handsome head held high, and above it, a mass of dark hair jiggling like a chanticleer's comb.

Back behind us in the dark, Wally Stewart, who can get a lot out of a tenor saxophone, played "I Left My Heart in San Francisco." Played by anyone this is a good tune, but Wally does something special to it. That night he shook it alive. It was as if his tenor seized the melody in its brassy teeth, and then from back in its reedy throat commenced to mutter about the blue and windy sea.

It must have been just after midnight when Captain Ponti came over and said that as it was such a gorgeous night we should get out on the river.

"I'd love it," said Dame Margot.

To say that what happened surprised me is putting it very mildly, but then I am constantly being surprised by the ways of the western world.

Leo disappeared. He returned with a flashlight, which

he pointed out of a terrace window, obviously making some sort of signal to someone on the water. A boat eased in out of the shadows and nosed alongside the narrow deck beneath the night club's terrace.

"Please, let's go aboard," said Captain Ponti.

A man in uniform helped us into the craft, and in the pale moonlight I saw, to my additional surprise, that the uniform was that of a London policeman.

"I must be mistaken," I said to myself.

At our feet waiters from the club placed a box, and I received a third surprise. It was a crate of champagne. The motor muttered into action and we slowly nosed out into the middle of the Thames and headed downstream, gliding past familiar buildings—the dark Houses of Parliament with the moon face of Big Ben above them, New Scotland Yard, the Savoy Hotel, and nearer the Pool of London, Southwark Cathedral, London Bridge, Tower Bridge, and just beyond, the ancient Tower of London.

We chugged along to the delightful sound of popping champagne corks and clinking glasses.

It was an unforgettable evening, especially for someone brought up in the conventional, almost prudish, atmosphere of a Communist society. In Moscow we had taken night rides on the Moskva River, winding through Moscow as the Thames does through London, but they were on the regular public well-regulated excursion boats that ply the river with large regimented parties. I asked no question that night on the Thames, but we certainly seemed to be aboard a police boat, a policeman in uniform at the wheel and another in blue standing near us, apparently to prevent any of us from tumbling overboard. We remained fairly upright, but I was enjoying myself so much that I do not believe I would have minded anything.

When at last we drew up at the River Club, I thanked the officer who had been so kind in pointing out the buildings

along the river, for on our return we had chugged upstream
as far as Putney.

"You're entirely welcome, ma'am," he said. With a smile
he added, "I only hope that you're not so grateful as to
also thank the Commissioner of Police."

Inside the club, Leo led us to his private apartment.
More champagne arrived, and the temperature rose several
degrees. Although she had danced an arduous ballet, Margot was lively, fresh, and enjoying it all. I supposed we had
been about eight people on the boat, and in the bright
lights of Leo's quarters I saw their faces clearly for the first
time. Three appeared to be foreigners and, I reasoned, probably from North Africa, where our host spent years of his
early life. In the fun, everyone seemed to perform a party
piece with the exception of a very quiet, dark, handsome
young man, and Dr. Arias, Dame Margot's dashing husband,
then Panamanian Ambassador to the Court of St. James's.
Unsmiling, the young man stood beside the serene envoy.

Captain Ponti had dressed himself in his Legionnaire's
uniform. The jacket failed to meet in front by at least six
inches, exposing no small area of his well-matted chest.
Kevin was doing an impersonation of the Hunchback of
Notre Dame, while Bobo seemed to be impersonating the
Statue of Liberty doing the Can-Can.

"Rather unusual behavior, don't you think?" I heard the
young man ask Dr. Arias.

"Yes, it is," replied Tito in his most austere diplomatic
voice. "They're all crazy." Whereupon—dinner jacket and
all—he executed a full front flip, landing squarely on his
feet.

This was too much for the young man.

He shook his head, and smiled one of the weakest smiles
I have ever seen.

"Who is he?" I whispered to Bobo.

"Oh, come on, Tamara."

"I don't know him. Who is he?"

"Crown Prince Mulay Hassan of Morocco."

"Oh," said I.

Today, of course, the young man is the King of Morocco. I walked over and spoke to Eddy.

"How did he ever get *him* here; I mean, out on the Thames and all that?"

"How did who get whom?"

"Leo get the Crown Prince?"

"Let me tell you something about Leo," said my husband. "That guy could telephone Calcutta and be able to speak to the man in the black hole."

But poor, brave, witty Tito. A political rival was soon to shoot him, leaving him almost totally paralyzed. With Margot's magnificent help and encouragement, and his great heart, he is making an astounding recovery.

27 Kevin McClory is the recognized leader of the International Order of Woodpeckers, a highly unesoteric, loosely organized group of extroverts. He contends that the human and animal world is made up of two primary generic types—the Woodpeckers and the Eggs.

Woodpeckers, he says, are individualistic in their behavior, philosophy, thoughts, and general outlook on life, the kind, tolerant, understanding owners of out-sized egos, and that while all eccentrics are Woodpeckers, all Woodpeckers are not eccentrics. They are contemptuous of greed, bigotry, cruelty, priggishness, pomposity, cant, disloyalty, and, of course, Eggs.

Eggs, Mr. McClory reasons, follow well-established and accepted behavior patterns. They are the conventional types whose reaction to any given stimulus is easily predictable. While they no doubt make safe partners, they are unexciting and dull as husbands, wives, boy friends and girl friends.

Lovers, he explains, are rarely Eggs. When they are, *their* lovers are Eggs.

I have seen Kevin enter a crowded room and in his mind's eye immediately separate, within a matter of moments, the Woodpeckers and the Eggs.

Woodpeckers, of course, have little difficulty in recognizing one another—and in spotting the Eggs with their all-too-obvious, monotonous, ovoid personalities.

Being an Irishman as well as a Woodpecker, McClory claims he was born in a donkey cart and I have never heard this disputed.

Shunning Eggs, but shunning them with a nice politeness, because he is instinctively a kind and polite man, he consorts almost exclusively with Woodpeckers, and knows them in large numbers all over the world.

Although my husband was in many things conservative, Kevin considered him a Woodpecker. I think this was because he engaged in a nightly dialogue with a dog. A French poodle named Ricky, the dog lived next door to us, and every evening, and sometimes on Saturday mornings, Ricky bounced into his garden, rushed along a tall and thick holly hedge, and started barking furiously at my husband.

Whatever Eddy Gilmore happened to be doing, he would put it aside at this barking through the holly hedge. Moving swiftly to our large mullioned window, he would fling it open and bark back at Ricky with the most dog-like noise I ever heard in my life, and I am convinced that it was the most dog-like bark that the dog next door had ever heard in his life. Oddly, our dog Mishka did not join in the barking. Mishka is, I think, an Egg. At home my husband liked to play the ukulele, which at his age and weight seemed undignified. However, I did not think his dog-barking dialogue undignified and this tolerant and unorthodox view of my husband's barking was, perhaps, why the chief Woodpecker considered me a Russian Woodpecker and not a Russian Egg.

Through Woodpecker McClory we had met many other Woodpeckers—Shirley MacLaine, Paddy Kennedy, Dame Margot Fonteyn and Tito Arias, the Maharanee of Cooch Behar, Trevor Howard, Sheamus Kelly, John Huston, Malcolm Arnold, and in spirit, but not in size, maybe the biggest Woodpecker of them all, the South African millionaire, John Schlesinger.

To assist the present Mrs. McClory in celebrating her twenty-first birthday as Bobo Sigrist, Schlesinger flew himself in a large and specially designed box from Johannesburg to London. This box was delivered to a night club, placed on Bobo's banquet table, and at the appropriate moment Mr. Schlesinger pushed up the box's top and sprang out to congratulate the beautiful birthday girl.

John came into our lives in Rome during the 1960 Olympic Games. Red-haired and close-cropped, a stubby man with lively, darting eyes, and quick nervous motions, he is the only human Woodpecker who resembles the feathered species. All he lacks is a long pointed beak, and if he possessed one, nothing made of wood would be safe in his company.

At the Olympic Games my husband had a very special assignment—to write about anything but sports. This might seem an extremely difficult thing to do for a period of three weeks, but not for Eddy Gilmore. In journalism he won his share of awards, the Pulitzer Prize, a special citation from Sigma Delta Chi, and the National Headliners Club Award, but I think he was proudest of a five-dollar bill he won as a bet—the wager being that he could not write an interesting—and I stress the word interesting—newspaper story fifteen hundred words long on how to tell a male goldfish from a female goldfish. So the Rome assignment was no hard chore.

I particularly liked a piece he did about Bricktop, then the proprietress of a night club on the Via Veneto. He said that for several generations she had been "helping the Romans burn their candles at both ends."

I met John Schlesinger under false pretenses.

While my husband was at the Olympic village—writing about the boyish enthusiasm shown by an amateur boxer and thoroughly nice young man named Cassius Clay as Eddy introduced him to Floyd Patterson, the world heavyweight champion—I was sitting in the sunshine of the Via Veneto with Bobo and Kevin.

A group of Rome's freelance photographers, the *paparazzi*, came loping along questing for prey. Kevin motioned them over and whispered something to one who seemed to be the leader. He had a long, thin frame, at the top of which was a small, round head. Hair sprouted from the man's skull and a dirty, unkempt beard from his chin.

On the table before Bobo and me rested two tall glasses.

In an overdone conspiratorial tone, Kevin began, "Obviously, you don't recognize those two girls."

"No."

"No, you don't. I can see you don't."

"Who are they?" asked the broom, his yellow eyes running up and down my figure from shoe to top hair as if he were unzipping me.

"The dark-haired girl is the Soviet sprint champion," said Kevin.

"No!"

"Yes, and the blonde is a breast stroker from the Bahamas' swimming team—"

The photographers swarmed about him and began cocking their cameras.

"Are you sure?" hissed one.

"Positive. They're my guests, as you can see, and I'm very disappointed in them. Look what they're doing. They're breaking training in the very worst way. They are drinking."

The lensmen scrambled over us, knocking one another about in their excitement. One, who spoke Russian, asked me, to a chorus of clicking, "Why aren't you with the Russian team?"

"Why should I be?"

"To practice. To train."

"Ha," said I with all the contempt I could summon, "I need no practice to outrun capitalists."

If I had known anything at all about athletics, this was the worst possible thing I could have said, for America's Wilma Rudolph was sprinting the spikes off all comers, including the best the Russians brought to Rome.

Obviously the Russian-speaking cameraman knew no more about sports than I.

"What's your name? The boys want your name."

"Maria," I told him.

"Maria what? Please."

"Maria Bezubova."

"Hold up your glasses," he said, "like you're taking a drink."

"I am taking a drink," I told him, swallowing a large portion of a completely non-alcoholic iced pineapple juice.

"Click, click, click, click," chatted the cameras.

Beside me Bobo was putting on the same outrageous performance. I looked at her just as she looked at me. Both of us struggled to choke back our laughter. Aware that I was unable to control myself, I stood up and hurried off down the street with the *paparazzi* in hot pursuit, snapping away as I swept along. I reached the Excelsior Hotel, ran up the steps and took refuge in the bar. The photographers did not follow. Perhaps the hotel barred them. The Excelsior is that sort of hotel.

It was a warm morning and I ordered another pineapple ice and was sipping away when The Associated Press's veteran photographer Jim Pringle, long stationed in Rome, hurried into the bar with the worried look of a man who has missed an important news picture. Making straight for me he said, "Are you the girl from the Russian Olympic team?"

"Yes," I told him. "The pineapple ice champion."

His handsome Irish face sagged.

"Come on, Jim Pringle. Don't you recognize me?"

"No. Yes," he gasped. "It's Tamara."

We were agreeing on how badly I had behaved when Bobo and Kevin entered.

"I'm leaving. Excuse me," said Jim. "I've got to go and undo all the mischief you've done. I've got to go tell those

poor chaps what's up. If I don't, every newspaper in Rome's
going to make suckers out of themselves."

With Kevin and Bobo was a short man with close-cropped,
reddish hair. He walked with quick, confident little steps
and his intelligent eyes moved this way and that, taking
in everything.

"I know a Woodpecker when I see one," I said to myself, "and this one must be a pilated Woodpecker. He's a
Woodpecker bigger than life."

I liked him instantly.

In an egalitarian world, he is one millionaire who enjoys
being one. There is another in Fulton, Alabama, one William
Harrigan. Unlike some I know, they have no complexes con-
cerning great wealth.

While John Schlesinger must be one of the last old-fashioned playboys, he has a deeply serious and religious side.
For one thing, South Africa's racial problems worry him and
he is one of those who try to do something about them.
I believe I am correct in saying that he is one of the
Republic's first businessmen to give an executive job to a
black man.

When the Olympics finished, John invited us to cruise
with him on his yacht, temporarily berthed at Salerno. From
there we sailed to Capri. For me the entire cruise and off-
ship-on-shore activities was one long, gay, slightly mad
party.

Outside Capri's largest hotel we lost John one morning.

"But we must find him," I told Eddy.

"What, me try to find John in Capri? Impossible. Let's
go into that lovely cool bar. Let him find us."

He did.

Within a few minutes he entered the bar astride a donkey.
I was aghast, but I seemed to be alone in my aghastment.
No one paid John or the animal the slightest attention. It
was not that he was in the habit of entering this particular
bar mounted on a donkey so much as Capri's acceptance of

almost any eccentric or eccentricity without the bat of an island eyelid. Over the years, Capri has adjusted itself to *everything*.

From his perch on the donkey's back, John ordered a drink. Quite politely the barman walked around one end of the bar and served him, but an Englishman sitting at a table for two looked up, saw the donkey almost sitting on him, and said to John, "I say, old boy, would you mind pointing that beast in the other direction?"

Later in the day we lost John again. It was dark, the yacht was his and we decided he must be located. Kevin and Eddy found him sitting at the top of a tree and coaxed him down.

As it was a hot moonlit night, we agreed to walk back to the boat through Capri's winding lanes. In seeking to keep their island neat, the authorities had placed a number of metal wastebaskets about the streets. These had skeleton frames of flat steel strips about two inches wide, and over this arrangement wire mesh was stretched. These trash baskets resembled those protective medical gadgets that doctors sometimes apply to the feet of gout sufferers, or to someone who has cracked a foot bone. This must have occurred to John too, because he halted before one of the baskets, stuffed his foot inside, and limped off with the contraption well wedged to his shoe.

A policeman stepped from the shadows and bore down on us. Arrest seemed imminent. The officer approached our host from the rear and just as he was about to stop him, John pointed to his basketed-foot and announced in his best and most distinct Italian, "War wound."

The policeman hesitated, stopped, smiled foolishly, shrugged his shoulders, and watched John with unmistakable admiration, as my Woodpecker friend disappeared into the night, the trash basket's metallic "clank, clank, clank" echoing through the sleepy streets.

Early in the following year John invited Eddy and me

to be his guests in South Africa, along with two of his American friends, Carl and Wilma Erbe.

"I want to show you the country," explained Mr. Schlesinger in a long cablegram.

He showed it to us all right—in a pair of private airplanes and a brace of Cadillacs. We visited every city and many small towns and seemed to meet everyone politically from the late Prime Minister Hendrik Verwoerd on down. It was a memorable trip and I shall always pray that South Africa's inhabitants, the whites, the blacks, and the coloreds, find some way of living together peacefully, profitably, and with dignity to all. It is such a beautiful land and so richly endowed.

We had a very unusual first day and first night.

Flying down from London we were assailed at Johannesburg Airport by John's unmistakable Woodpecker voice cackling upon us from a crowded balcony on the administration building. I believe the crowd had gathered to witness the departure of someone important from Johannesburg. Anyhow, several hundred persons flanked John and seemed to be watching him and waiting to hear and see what he was going to do.

They did not have long to wait.

As we happily hurried along the tarmac in the golden sun of South Africa's early February, our host greeted us with, "Yanks, go home!"

To my chagrin, several hundred people roared with laughter. I do not know who they were. They may have been only ordinary members of the crowds that haunt the spectator positions at international airports. On the other hand, John Schlesinger, chairman of the far-flung Schlesinger Organization, may have hired them the way the press agents of pop stars engage crowds to welcome their hairy heroes home to London Airport. Ours, however, was a welcome in reverse.

Mr. Schlesinger bristles with surprises.

He put us up in his lush apartment house in a quiet Johannesburg suburb. After a merry dinner, followed by a noisy party, we finally staggered wearily to bed.

The apartment house—one of several that he owns—was large and spacious, built around a grassy flowered court-yard. Each apartment had its own balconies, one looking out on the courtyard, the other over a street of expensive homes.

Being sensible, normal people, the occupants of the numerous other apartments retired long before we did. Suddenly—and by this time Eddy and I were in bed—the night's silence was shattered by John's voice.

Standing on his balcony in his dressing gown he, to our horror, called out to his sleeping tenants:

"My name is Eddy Gilmore. I'm an American who lives in London. Why don't you bastards pay more rent?"

Now happily married to a handsome Italian, John has calmed down.

I often wonder, however, if the occupants of Whitehall Court *did* pay more rent.

Dear John, you are one in ten million. Thank you for many things, but most of all for laughter.

28 "I've been insulted by beautiful women in my life," announced my husband one afternoon, "but never before by a female aged three."

"How's that?"

"Natasha. I've just taken her for a spin in the new car and she said to me, 'Papa, my feet won't touch the floor.' And I told her, 'Well, don't worry. At your age mine wouldn't either. Do you know that once upon a time I was just as small as you?'"

"And what did Natasha say to that?"

"That's just what I'm coming to. She said to me, 'Yes, I know. I've seen the picture of you when you were a little boy. It's on Mama's dresser.'"

Eddy looked as if he had seen a ghost.

"And then the child said to me in all her innocence, 'Papa, what did you do to your face?'"

"All right, go on," I told him.

"Go on? How can I go on when a child—my own child—tells me something like that? I think it's deflated me more than anything I've ever heard in my life."

"What did you do?" I asked.

"Why, I terminated the ride. That's what I did. I turned the car around and brought her home."

"Honey, how long have you been living in rented houses and furnished apartments in foreign countries?"

"What's that got to do with the traumatic experience I've just been through?"

"Nothing. I was only changing a painful subject, changing

it to something I've been wanting to talk about for a long time."

"Well, let's see. I've been a foreign correspondent for, er, twenty-two years."

"Always in rented quarters?"

"Always."

"I don't know about you, but I'd like a place of my own. I know that Vicki and Susanna would too."

"Where do you want to buy one?"

"In London, if possible."

"Well, I don't think it is possible, not the kind of house I want to live in."

"Well, let's start looking."

For nearly six months we spent every weekend inspecting London houses. Those we liked were too expensive.

While our solicitor (lawyer) was exchanging a series of baffling letters with the owners' solicitors, we went again to the United States. Every third year The Associated Press charitably and wisely gives their foreign correspondents a home leave; that is, the company pays their transportation and that of their families back to the States and then, after a vacation there, it foots the return passage to the foreign post.

Up until a few years ago I had never been farther west than Mobile, Alabama. Now as I write this my westernmost penetration has been Indianapolis. While Indianapolis is a delightful city and contains four charming friends, Eugene and Jane Pulliam and Tamara and Ernest Jacques, it is hardly the Wild West, and that is where I thought I was going when I heard our destination was Indiana. I still long to push my western frontiers beyond Mobile and Indianapolis. It is one of my dreams.

In Alabama—the state that adopted me—live some of our closest friends, Chuck and Alice Hohenberg, Joe and Mary Lib Callaway, Muriel Lewis, and the brothers McGowin. One of Eddy's oldest and dearest friends was the late Arthur

Lewis. With Arthur gone, visits to Selma will never be the same.

The McGowins make up one of America's most unusual and attractive families. The four brothers—Floyd, Earl, Julian, and Nicholas—all graduated from the University of Alabama and then went on to Oxford. Until 1966 they owned (with other branches of their family) and operated the W. T. Smith Lumber Company, a highly successful lumber manufacturing business with some 220,000 acres largely of pine land around its plant at Chapman, Alabama. They also have other interests.

The various boards on which the McGowins serve, with sagacity and distinction, include that of a large railway and Eddy said the reason they got on that directorship is to enable the trains to stop at Chapman, a tiny town in Butler County.

The McGowins dismissed Eddy's theory as nonsense, but he resolutely clung to his view, pointing out that trains began to halt at Chapman, whereas they raced through with indecent haste and noise before the board of directors included the McGowins, or at least one or two of them.

Back in the days before the train began stopping at Chapman, a nightly procedure of the W. T. Smith Lumber Company was to station one of its employees alongside the tracks. As the trains roared past, a bag of mail for the timber operators would be hurled off into the dark. The employee would then try to locate it, and if successful, take it to the company offices.

Then, and as far as I know now, the local telephone company was a private business, not a public utility, and the president of this snug pocket of rugged individualism was convinced that telephone calls should be restricted to daylight hours; that the night was for sleeping, not talking. For this reason he resolutely discouraged the use of the telephone after dark.

"Mr. Charlie," began the mail bag collector on this fateful evening, "gimme me depot in Greenville, please sir."

Whether Mr. Charlie made his decision after long thought, or whether it was on the spur of the moment, I do not know —and neither do the McGowins—but Mr. Charlie was fed up. He could not have been more explicit, for to the request to be connected with the depot in Greenville he said:

"I ain't a-gonner do it!" breaking the connection from Chapman and going back to bed.

In addition to being sound businessmen, the brothers McGowin are musical, having a string quartet of their own. Floyd, the elder of the McGowins, is the only man I know whose house contains a room specially built for use by a family string ensemble.

29 Britain has many unusual organizations. For one there is the Flat Earth Society. Its members are convinced that the world is flat and that geographers, astronomers, and other scientists who contend the world is round are misguided squares perpetuating a gigantic hoax on the inhabitants of this planet.

There is also the Anglo-Texan Society. Its membership is composed of Britons who are in love with Texas and Texans. For years its president was the late Lord Bossom. After an Anglo-Texan dinner in the august House of Lords, my husband and I, with others, were invited to Lord Bossom's magnificent town house on Carlton House Terrace.

Sir Alfred, as he then was, asked me point-blank, "Did you ever hear the story of Sir Winston Churchill and me? No? Then you stand where you are—Hughes, bring this lady a drink—Well, you see, Churchill happened to be present in the House of Commons when I made my maiden speech. When I sat down he nudged another member and asked, 'Who's that man?'

"'New member. Fellow named Bossom.'

"'What name?'

"'Bossom, sir.'

"'How do you spell it?'

"'B o double s o m—Bossom.'

"'Bossom,' said Churchill, rolling the name around on his tongue. 'Why, it's neither one thing nor the other, is it?'"

Lord Bossom was very fond of this story about himself. This is one of the things I like about the English. They laugh so readily and easily at themselves. I say English and not British, for I am not sure that Scots, Welshmen, and Ulstermen are given to telling stories against themselves. It must be a part of their built-in, bred-in, or drilled-in modesty. Of all the people I have ever known the English are by far the most self-effacing, habitual mockers of themselves.

Now how did I, a Russian-born naturalized American, happen to be at a dinner of the Anglo-Texan Society? It was because Michael Bryceson, the perpetual chairman of the Texas-lovers, is our solicitor. This, and I suppose the fact that my husband was always lecturing in Texas. I said lecturing *in* not *at* Texas. Only Heaven and Eddy's agent W. Colston Leigh know how many times and places he spoke in Texas, but I recall dates in Dallas, Houston, Beaumont, Corpus Christi, Denton, Pampa, Wichita Falls, Austin, and College Station.

In any case, by the time my husband had finished lecturing in Texas and a lot of other places on his home leave, the Chairman of the Anglo-Texan Society in London had tied up the loose ends and Old Porch House was ours.

East Grinstead, in the county of Sussex, is thirty-five miles south of London on the A22 which the British Ministry of Transport quaintly designate a major highway. It is, of course, nothing of the sort. It is a narrow, winding, up-hill-down-hill road that has been where it is for a long, long time. The roads of England, it has been said, were laid out by drunken shepherds following crippled cows, which seems a logical assumption I say. Old Porch House is in East Grinstead. It could hardly be more in it, for it's in High Street. It also stands on the highest hill between London and Brighton on the English Channel. As I do not drive an automobile, and I seriously doubt if I could ever learn to drive one, residing in the very center of an old market town has its advantages. I step out of my front door and within a distance of several hundred yards there is my butcher, greengrocer, tailor, florist, fruit shop, wine dealer, gunsmith, milliner, bank, beauty shop, jeweler, antique dealer, pedicurist, supermarket, Woolworth's, hardware store, newspaper and magazine dealer, book shop, druggist, optician, doctor, filling station, car dealer, record shop, post office, television specialist, sweater shop, two hotels, three pubs and the parish church. When my husband worked in London all day, and with the Church of England's convent school of St. Agnes and St. Michael within walking distance for the children, I found Old Porch House a highly convenient home.

One might think that living in the center of a busy English town is uncomfortable, too urban and noisy, but here again the house is unique. Once you step through our fortress-like Tudor front door, you are in the country. From our large mullioned window in the drawing room there are broad and uninterrupted views of the Ashdown Forest four miles away. The vista is as rural as a haystack, or a rail fence with not so much as a single telephone post, electric pylon, or automobile to be seen. On clear days you can pick out individual sheep grazing in a meadow, a distance of some three and a half miles from our garden.

The last three people to be burned at the stake in England met their hideous fate a few yards up High Street from Old Porch House, and are buried in the adjacent churchyard of St. Swithun's. Our vicar, the Reverend H. C. F. Copsey, says with a wink that Sussex was the last county in England to become Christian, and to his way of thinking it is still half-pagan.

In and around East Grinstead live many friends, and two of the kindest and most delightful of these are Tom and Fleur Cowles Meyer. During the week they reside in one of London's most elegant apartments, followed by weekends at their jewel-like Sussex house, Great Surries.

The whole world seems to visit Great Surries—kings, queens, prime ministers, cabinet members, film stars, authors, architects, great surgeons, commentators, ambassadors, and others.

One Sunday at lunch there we were presented to Queen Frederika of Greece and her daughter, Princess Irene. In conversation with my husband the Queen related how the day before, she and the Princess were actually chased down a side street and into a cul-de-sac by part of a group demonstrating outside Claridge's against the imprisonment in Greece of a Greek Communist, accused and convicted of terrorism.

With every sentence of Queen Frederika's graphic description of what must have been for her and her daughter a frightening experience, I watched my husband's mounting excitement. You know, the old fire horse at the smell of smoke business.

Not a word of what had happened to the royal visitors had, up to then, appeared in any British newspaper and, as far as I know, in no other publication. The Queen and her daughter had maintained a dignified silence, but, as Eddy realized, a story of this nature never remains unprinted for long.

"Ma'am," he asked, "may I use these facts as a news story?"

She seemed surprised and explained that she wanted to give no impression of seeking or giving an interview.

"But ma'am, this is a legitimate news story. It's sure to come out soon. The public should know about such things."

After much discussion, she relented. Then double-checking various facts with Scotland Yard and an eyewitness, Eddy cabled the story to the United States and other parts of the world. Relayed back to Britain from New York twelve hours later, it made headlines in London papers. Asked in the House of Commons how such a thing could happen to supposedly guarded royal visitors to England, a cabinet member denied any such incident had taken place. The following day, however, he got up, apologized for misleading the House, and apologized on behalf of the British Government to the Queen and the Princess and said the newspaper reports were accurate.

Meeting Queen Frederika and Princess Irene led to many happy occasions, at least for us. A person whom I admire and respect, the Queen has, to my deep conviction, been the victim of a cruel leftwing conspiracy. In their efforts to destroy order in Greece certain elements within the country, and others beyond its frontiers, seek first to bring down the royal family. They go about this by attacking Queen Frederika because of her German birth. What her enemies never seem to point out is that while she was born a German princess, she is also a direct descendant of Queen Victoria and underwent most of her schooling in England. With her husband, the late King Paul of the Hellenes, she was a close friend of that great man, Jan Christian Smuts, South African Prime Minister and ardent opponent of Nazism and its adherents. For her bravery, the Queen was decorated after firsthand participation in the Greek civil war when the country was all but lost to the Communists.

While writing a story on the Greek royal family, my husband was dining at Tatoi Villa outside Athens one balmy November night. Present were King Paul, Queen Frederika, and Princess Irene. After dinner the four of them were having coffee in the drawing room when an excited servant rushed in and babbled something in Greek to the King. King Paul's face seemed to drain of blood as he said to Eddy, "I'm afraid I've just been given some terrible news. Your President has been murdered."

My husband jumped to the telephone and through his office in Athens confirmed the terrible truth.

"We Americans," he said, "can be so violent."

"You have no monopoly on violence," commented the King. "In our civil war I saw violence that sickened me. Unfortunately, there seem to be times when violence comes out in us all. No, I know America and Americans. Violence is not one of your national characteristics."

Members of the Greek royal family were friends and admirers of President and Mrs. John F. Kennedy. Mrs. Kennedy and her sister, Princess Lee Radziwill, had but a few weeks before been guests at Tatoi Villa. At the dinner that my husband attended the Queen went out of her way to stress with what pleasure she looked forward to a visit early in the coming year to the White House.

Like presidents, kings too live in the shadow of assassination. King Paul's grandfather, King George I, was assassinated on March 18, 1913.

As my husband and the King discussed the appalling tragedy at Dallas, Eddy asked if assassination was not a specter that automatically associates itself with the occupant of any throne. Eddy made a note of the reply: "It's just one of those things you must never worry about. You learn to live with it and in living with it, it slowly recedes from your conscious, if not unconscious, thoughts."

Stunned by President Kennedy's death he seemed for a few minutes to be thinking out loud, recalling how after he and his brother, King George II—born in the villa in which he now sat—once returned from a drive in a carriage and a groom discovered a bullet freshly embedded in the harness of one of the horse.

His eyes remained closed as he said, "We had been driving through large crowds in Athens. You know we never learned whether someone had fired the bullet at my brother the King, or at me."

In less than four months this good, kind, and wise man was to die. His only son Constantine—whom the King had personally tutored in the uneasy and dangerous profession of Balkan kingsmanship—succeeded. He is a man with rare courage and dignity in one so young.

He is beset by sharp and deep divisions among the

politicians, the armed forces, the people of Greece's space-age democracy.

The Greeks invented democracy—*demokratis*, from *demos* "the people" and *kratos* "rule."

What tragic irony should Greece become a country where democracy is destroyed.

30 For the last decade (all through this book I have been aching to use this word, which I have only recently learned) my husband covered Europe's royal weddings: Princess Margaret's to that gifted young London photographer Antony Armstrong-Jones, the Duke of Kent's to Katharine Worsley, King Baudouin to Dona Fabiola Fernanda Maria de las Victorias Antonia Adelaida de Mora y Aragon, Prince Albert Felix Humbert Theodore Christian Eugene Marie of Liége to Donna Paola Margherita Maria Antonia Ruffo di Calabria, Mr. Angus Ogilvy's to Princess Alexandra, and, of course, that earlier one of the Prince of Monaco to Miss Grace Kelly. So when the engagement of King Constantine to Princess Anne-Marie of Denmark was announced, Eddy's New York office asked him to go to Athens for that one.

As he said, "The only proper way to cover a royal wedding is as a guest," and I am inclined to think he was right. Through Queen Frederika we received an invitation to her son's nuptials and to other parties connected with the event, including the ball to out-ball all balls—held in the spacious gardens of the royal palace almost in the heart of the Greek capital.

As the most unroyal of guests, our invitation directed us to be at the palace at 9 P.M., while the large assemblage of kings, queens, princes, and princesses and President Johnson's daughter Lynda Bird was leisurely to arrive thirty minutes later, after the hoi polloi had been assigned to its places. My husband and I had on the correct clothes, for which I was mercifully thankful. He wore a short, tailored white linen, silk-lined jacket, white tie, and black silk trousers with a nice strip of inky silk braid down the sides. My dress was light blue, a blue that I hoped was Mediterranean blue.

"Why Mediterranean blue?" asked Eddy.

"To be the same color as the sea down there," I replied.

"You'd better have another look at your map," he told me.

"You mean you don't like my gown of Mediterranean blue?"

"I love it. I was afraid you were going to show up in Peloponnesian pink."

My gloves were kid and very long, the shoes blue and American. I adore jewels and my proudest possession is an aquamarine surrounded by thirty-seven small diamonds which I brought out of Russia. I topped this off with a regal tiara, graciously lent me by a friend and neighbor, the Marchioness of Aberdeen.

To my eternal mortification, once again I was late, so late that Eddy gave me not just his angry cherub look, but his awfully angry cherub look. We shot from the front door of the Athens Hilton—at which a number of the wedding guests were staying—but not where the royal guests were housed. They were downtown closer to the palace.

In a scrambled combination of atrocious Greek, French, and English my furious spouse instructed a taxi driver to take us to the Royal Palace as quick as he could get us there. The driver goofed the first part of his instructions, but he won full marks for the latter. As the downtown streets were roped off for the ball, our cabby had a clear run. Even in heavy traffic the taxi men of Athens are speedsters. With the thoroughfares this evening virtually empty of vehicles on this special occasion, we swept along at something between fifty and sixty miles an hour, slowing down only when we raced into the actual downtown sector. To my surprise a tremendous crowd was on hand, packed solid on the sidewalks. It was a beautiful moonlit night. It even smelled beautiful. Great searchlights fingered the cloudless skies and other giant-sized projectors washed backward and forward over the human seas. We moved through packed corridors of men, women, and children but at last we began slowing down.

As Eddy had earlier handed the driver a royal insignia which he proudly and wisely stuck to his windshield, our taxi was being waved on by every policeman and soldier along the way. And it was that royal crest, of course, that admitted our dusty old taxi to a stately procession of slowly moving Rolls-Royces, Cadillacs, and other expensive cars. I almost panicked when I saw that up ahead, about seventy-five yards away, these same limousines were picking up—not letting out—men and women dressed as we were, the men in tailored short white jackets and the women in long gowns and tiaras.

Our taxi came to a halt in front of a floodlit building which literally bristled with television and still cameras. Pressing behind the photographers were hundreds of cheering Athenians. As I stepped from our cab the lights partially blinded me, but I felt my feet on something nice, smooth and soft. Looking down I saw it was a red carpet. I mean a real red carpet. After paying the driver Eddy followed me into the glittering foyer of this building. At that moment I saw Queen Juliana and Prince Bernhard of the Netherlands. What startled me was that they were walking toward the door through which we had only just entered.

"Now I know something's wrong," I whispered.

I made a quick curtsy, Eddy a bow, and we got out of their royal way. Moving fast, my husband approached a dignified-looking uniformed man standing stiffly at attention along one wall of the foyer and explained our predicament.

"Oh, sir," explained the man, "you want the Royal Palace."

"What's this?"

"This, sir, is the King George Hotel. You see, it's reserved for royalty during the wedding."

"But how are we going to get through that mob outside? I mean, how are we going to get through them to get to the palace?"

I suppose it was because of his long years as a foreign correspondent, dealing with officialdom in all sorts of lands, but Mr. Gilmore had a sure instinct of nearly always approaching the right man in tight spots, and this one was tight.

"Just who are you, sir?" asked the man in uniform.

"Guests to tonight's ball," said my husband producing the invitations embossed with the golden crest of the Hellenic dynasty.

"I'll tell you what we'll do, sir. As you can see, motorcars are arriving outside every minute or so for the royal guests. We'll just put you and Milady in one of them."

That is exactly what happened.

To a burst of hand-clapping we were ushered into a most handsome limousine, piloted by a most handsome uniformed chauffeur. We purred off slowly and majestically to the cheering of thousands!

As we neared the palace itself, and the streets narrowed, the human walls actually seemed to press against our car. The people began chanting something. Over his shoulder the driver said:

"Pardon me, Your Highness. They want to see you."

With that he switched on the interior lights.

"My God," gasped my husband, quickly turning them off.

"They want to *see* you and your lady, Your Highness," said the driver in a pleading voice. "They want to see whom they're cheering."

The light came on again, exposing us to the stares of thousands. I mean thousands, too.

"We can't let this go on," muttered Eddy in Russian. "This is embarrassingly presumptuous."

He said presumptuous in English, for I am sure he did not know that word in Russian.

Slowly the car moved ahead.

I went along with the whole charade, smiling and waving at the cheering people of Athens, but my untitled cavalier from the Deep South—generally an unashamed extrovert—seemed to be trying to do a vanishing act in the corner of the deeply upholstered car.

"Do you know who they think I am?" he asked.

"Who?"

"Just listen to them."

I listened. There could be no mistake. Even in Greek I could recognize, loud and clear, the name—*Farouk.*

More, far more embarrassment awaited us.

Our driver stopped at the circular end of the real palace's driveway, and a uniformed servant waiting there, whipped open the door of the car. The Grand Chamberlain loomed over us. He gave me a deep bow. I have not the faintest idea who he thought we were, but unmistakably we were getting the royal treatment.

Bowing and smiling, he led us to a wide terrace that over-looked acres of palace lawn, illuminated by strategically placed floodlights. I am sure I have never viewed a more impressive piece of real estate. A big lemon-colored moon hung almost overhead. In front of us led a wide and long flight of marbled steps, and down at the foot of those steps, standing in respectful silence in landscaped gardens, several hundred guests were waiting—prime ministers, foreign min-isters, cabinet ministers, ambassadors, government officials, shipping magnates, diplomats, bankers, and their ladies.

We were put into the royal procession, just behind the King and the Queen of the Belgians and—I am too chagrined to name them—just before an ex-king and his ex-queen.

With about ten feet between each couple we moved off down the marbled steps. The ambassadors and the others standing so obediently on each side of the broad garden walk bowed deeply as we moved past them.

"What in the name of the good God do we do?" I asked in Russian. I was genuinely alarmed to be placed—by mistake, of course—in this exalted procession.

"I'd like to run," said Eddy through his teeth, "but it's too late now. Just smile, hold your head high, look straight ahead and try to act as if you belong here."

I riveted my alarmed eyes on the back of King Baudouin's neck, and walked on like a person going to her execution. Out of the edges of my eyes I took in all too well the deep bows and the curtsies.

"Any moment now," whispered my husband, "somebody's going to call out, 'Gilmore, you phony, what are you doing *there?*'"

Looking to neither the right nor the left, I kept a frozen smile on my face. To my indescribable relief no one spotted us, or if he or she did, he or she mercifully kept his or her mouth shut.

At last the ordeal was over. We had reached a long, crescent-like, beautifully decorated pavilion. This was at the very end of the garden through which we had walked. Ranged alongside one another in chairs within the open pavilion were members of the Greek and Danish royal families.

Spotting us, Queen Frederika motioned us forward. My knees actually trembled as we climbed the carpeted steps to be presented by Queen Frederika to King Constantine and the truly beautiful Princess he was to wed.

I was certain that everyone was looking at us; that someone was sure to cry out about our presence in that royal procession, but no. Having seen the Queen greet and present us, I presume that other royals—if they noticed us at all—presumed that we belonged where we were.

The band struck up a tune and I found myself dancing. Crown Princess Irene swept by with a titled partner, recognized us, excused herself from her Prince, and gave us a most gracious and warming middle-of-the-dance-floor greeting.

Oh, yes. There is one thing more. Some sort of subtle segregation seemed to prevail. The prime ministers, the generals, the ambassadors, and so on, were using a bigger dance floor about one hundred yards up the garden from the smaller, more private dance floor being used by us "royals."

Throughout this fairy-tale evening in that sublimely illuminated garden, dancing to Lev's wonderful music, no one asked us who we were or how we happened to be where we were. No one even requested a view of our invitation.

On many occasions I have felt a long way from Ulitsa Krasina in Moscow. I never felt more so than on this evening.

The Associated Press, incidentally, had a very firsthand, detailed account of the royal ball from a unique royal point of view.

31 Life in a small English town is fun.
Of course one misses the mammoth supermarkets
of the United States with their fresh vegetables, the fruit so
fat, ripe and pretty that it looks like fruit imitating fruit,
the wide variety of wheat products, and the meat. Oh, what
meat.

Most things American blow eastward across the Atlantic
and eventually reach Britain, but not yet those cello-
phaned cornucopias of abundance, blessed with parking
space. We have supermarkets, of course, but there are none
around East Grinstead, Sussex, in any way comparable to
the ones to be found in a similar sized state-side town.

I also long for the efficient American dry cleaning estab-
lishments with their rapid service. To get a silk evening gown
properly cleaned in Britain I have found that I must take
it to London and hand it in at Harrod's, one of the world's
finest department stores. Missing from my life too are the
easily contained and easily maintained American gadgets
that do make life easier in the kitchen. When one does find
modern gadgets in Britain they are often highly priced.

But—there are features of shopping in rural England that
I do find most pleasant. The greengrocer knows you. So does
the butcher, the baker, the jeweler, the antique dealers,
the fishmonger, the news agent, and all their employees.
There is a warm intimate friendliness in a small English
town and not too much hurry. The shopkeepers and their
assistants have time to talk to you, and they do not try to sell

you their wares. They take the attitude of being there to serve you should you just happen to make a purchase.

With a visiting American I once walked into a shop that sells good and expensive jewelry. My friend fell in love with a ring. She asked the price. It was in the neighborhood of two hundred pounds, about 560 dollars.

"Oh, Tamara, I love it," she said, "but as you know, I'm going home tomorrow and my money's run low."

"Eddy can probably dig it up for you," I said, but there may have been just a tiny tone of apprehension in my voice for Mr. Gilmore was not in the habit of digging up, especially at short notice, the equivalent of 560 dollars to lend to a young girl on the eve of her departure for the United States.

"Oh, madame," said the jeweler, "don't give it a thought. If you like it, take it and you can send me the money from America."

"But suppose my father won't let me keep it?"

"Then send it back to us, madame."

"Are you sure this will be all right? You don't even know my name."

"But you can give it to us."

"Well," said my friend, "I'm sure of one thing, I never saw anyone as trusting as you are."

"We learn to be great judges of character in this business, madame."

My friend took the ring, flew off the next day to her homeland, showed the ring to her father and told him the price and how she had been trusted.

"Here's a check," said her father, "but that guy must be in love with you or nuts."

"He's neither, Daddy. He's an English gentleman."

In the smaller shops of a small town nothing seems to raise one's status with shopkeepers so much as an appearance on television, or on the state-supported British Broadcasting Corporation's excellent noncommercial radio services.

The whole Gilmore family has been on TV for one reason or another a number of times—and it truly helps in the shops. I don't know why it is, but a great many people in England seem to like identifying themselves with what they see on what they call the Gogglebox. An expert on human behavior must have an easy explanation for this. I do not.

Living in a cottage near us when we moved into our Old Porch House we found a Mr. George White, born in bleak County Norfolk many years ago. He is one of the most cheerful humans I have ever known. We more or less inherited him as a gardener, open fireplace layer and log splitter. Small, wiry and in his late seventies, George White was a dispatch rider in World War I, and for all his sunny disposition, a tough little man. To survive he had to be, for he was born on a farm which was constantly air-conditioned by the chilling—even in high summer—winds blowing off the nearby North Sea. His first job in life was at the age of thirteen when he became a mobile scarecrow, or bird-frightener, at a weekly salary of one shilling which, in those days, was about twenty-five cents. George White walked three miles to his work six days a week, marched the fields all day long frightening the avaricious birds, then trudged the three miles home, often in the dark and snow.

"Don't ever talk to me about the good old days," he often says. "Cor, the good old days are today."

The former owners of our house addressed George White simply as "White." In England this is the standard form of address for gardeners, chauffeurs and others in domestic employment, but my husband and I never became accustomed to it. Only with considerable self-discipline was he able to break himself from the charming habit of the American South of addressing persons his own age and older as "ma'am" and "sir."

To us George White was always Mr. White, and he always will be.

Actually—as the English say—actually, when we first

moved in, we did not know what his first name was. He was introduced to us simply as, "And this is White. He gardens."

On our move to Sussex from London we brought our black cat George. Though born in the Cotswolds, George the cat grew up from kittenhood in the penthouse and is, by disposition, a city boy. From literally living in the clouds and recklessly strolling the edges of balconies on the roof of a tall apartment house, George did not at first find life on the ground in Sussex very exciting. Or perhaps he found it too exciting. Whatever his state of mind it took him months to settle down. He wandered often, which meant we were constantly looking for him and calling him at all hours of the day and night.

One morning our next door neighbor, Dr. Francis Briggs, came in and after a few puffs on his pipe, asked, "Do you know White's Christian name?"

We said we did not know it.

"I happened to know it because he's a patient of mine. You probably don't know it, but every time you call your cat George, White pops his head out of his back door. He's a trifle deaf, you know, but not so deaf that he doesn't hear your strident calls for 'George!' He's quite mystified. I'm afraid he's mistaking your calls for your cat for the supernatural. Like so many people in Sussex, believes in ghosts and all that."

"Could all this be possible?" asked my husband.

"I'll assure you it is," replied the doctor.

"You'll forgive me if I give it a test in your presence."

Opening our back door, the one that looks out on Mr. White's long narrow garden, Eddy called in a loud voice, "George, George."

Sure enough, the gardener's door opened and out stepped Mr. White, looking not in the direction of our house, but up in the soft Sussex sky.

Closing the door softly, Eddy said to Dr. Briggs and

me, "I'll bet you that comes from all those birds in his youth."

Another neighbor and friend in East Grinstead is the Reverend Harry Copsey, vicar of our parish church, St. Swithun's. A regular feature of the English summer in the country is the garden fete, organized to raise money for churches and other good causes, and these fetes are invariably opened by some local person of distinction—or notoriety.

To my surprise and incomprehension I, Tamara Gilmore, late arrival in a town which was inhabited years before the birth of Christ, was asked by the vicar to officially open the fete.

Bazaars and fetes are opened with speeches, and when I told Eddy I needed one, he agreed to help me compose it. Knowing me, he kept it short, and I set about trying to memorize it. I thought I knew my speech, but I had dreadful misgivings about making it. For one thing, I had never made a speech in public.

The day of the fete arrived, and for a change, the weather was kind. A warm sun smiled down from an almost cloudless sky and there was no wind whipping in from the west as it usually whips in on our high hill. Many of the ladies wore flowery summer dresses and hats. They made a pretty picture as they assembled on the green lawn.

The moment came for me to open the festivities. Calling for silence, the vicar introduced me, graciously as is his way. The cameras of the photographers from the two local and vigorously competitive weekly newspapers clicked away and I began speaking.

As I forgot a great deal of what I was supposed to say, my address was shorter by far than I had intended. The applause was polite and after it was over a pretty, well-dressed woman came up to me and said, "May I congratulate you on the best and shortest speech I've ever heard at one of these things, and I've been to a few in my day."

"Thank you," I told her. "Thank you very much, but did you understand it?"

"Not a word," she said with a sweet smile, moving off into the ocean of summer hats.

Two days later the *Courier* and the *Observer* appeared with flattering accounts of the fete and my speech. I am unable to remember which paper it was, but one of them headlined its reporter's account of my best-spoken English:

TAMARA OPENS FETE
SPEAKS IN RUSSIAN

32 If I had to choose between the two it is my mother in Russia, not Mother Russia, that draws me back to Moscow. By this I do not mean any lack of affection for Russia. On the contrary, I love her too.

What is it that creates in most of us such a fondness for our homelands? Putting aside the more obvious nationalistic reasons, such as pride of accomplishment, admiration of historical feats of gallantry, contributions to the humanities and to science; is it not true that we have strong feelings for the places—countries, cities and even towns and villages—where happy memories far overbalance the unhappy ones, where on returning to them we know we will find people whose love and friendship we cherish?

In the United States, England, and in other lands, people often ask me if my family *does* not long to join me in the West. Truthfully, I tell them "No."

For those who are not Russian, it must be hard to accept the fact that citizens of the Soviet Union—many of whom have suffered through two world wars, a revolution, famines, and the long cruel years of Stalin's dictatorship with their inhuman purges, debasement of dignity and self respect—do not yearn to flee to the West. I am quite sure that many do. I am also certain that should the Soviet authorities open their frontiers tomorrow and abolish the exit visa system, a large proportion of the people would remain where they are. As this book is neither a sociological, political nor psychological treatise on the Russian people, may I say, that to my mini-mind, there are some very simple but valid reasons for this.

Speaking nothing but his native language, or dialect, what would a peasant do in the highly developed technology of American agriculture? How would a Tadjik, or Kazhak, employ himself in a Pennsylvania steel mill, or a Kalmuck be happy in the great open spaces of Texas and Arizona? Could an Uzbek cotton grower make his way and be happy in Mississippi? A Georgian wine grower might find a place for himself in the sophisticated vineyards of New York State or California, but I doubt it, just as much as I question whether the average Muscovite—without friends or relatives in the United States—would be happy, or could earn his way in Kansas City.

"Ah, but Russians have done it," some will say. This is quite true, but were not most of these immigrants refugees from the revolution, aristocrats, members of the middle class, or Jews whose long persecution in Tsarist Russia conditioned them against hardship, adversity and a life with the odds weighed heavily against them?

With an American husband, or to a lesser extent, perhaps an American wife, it might be possible for a middle-aged Soviet citizen today to make for himself or herself a happy, normal life in the western democracies with their competitive economies. Of the small number of Russian girls who married Americans, Britons and Frenchmen during the last war, and like me, managed to leave the USSR, most of the ones I know seem quite happy in their new homelands—but not all of them—far from it, in fact. Two have lost their minds, another in her bewildering unhappiness, turned to dope.

I realize that this is a cliché, but like many clichés, a truism; that everything in life being relative you usually do not worry about the things of which you know little or nothing. Among Russia's two hundred and thirty millions, scattered across one-fifth of the earth's surface, there are many who have never seen an American, and the United States is a far away place as remote as the moon. To move to America would no more occur to them than an urge to rocket to the moon.

Among Moscow's intelligentsia (incidentally, it was a Russian, Feodor Dostoyevsky, in *The Devils,* who invented the word intelligentsia) I have heard painters, writers, and musicians long out loud for the artistic freedoms of the West, but I have not heard many of them say they would exchange their somewhat exalted positions in their homeland for creative liberties elsewhere.

I am more than aware that Russian mothers and housewives yearn for spacious clean apartments with wonderful labor-saving devices, and I am convinced that large numbers might, on first thought, consider exchanging their way of life for a place where these things are readily available. On thinking again though, I have had them—in talks with me in Moscow—say, "But what about all that crime and violence in America? We hear that in some American cities women and girls are afraid to leave their homes after dark —that they hesitate even to take their dogs for a stroll at night."

That this is sometimes true, I have to admit, and, reluctantly, I have had to admit that there are schoolteachers in some big American cities who live in fear of their students and that some are actually attacked and murdered by those they are teaching.

While I affirm these ugly features of life in a western democracy I point out also that the man who, for generations, once ruled their lives once attacked his schoolteacher, who was a priest at that.

"Oh," they say, "but that was Stalin."

Russia is in no way free from violence and crime, but it is freer than some western nations.

Then there is this terrible dope traffic and addiction. Again, in the Soviet Union the use of dangerous drugs is not unheard of. The opportunities of easily obtaining drugs are rare; yet, they are bought and there are addicts. Knowing the Russian character, I am unable to say what the incident of addiction would be were heroin, cocaine, morphine, and some of the other in-vogue drugs be as easy to come by as they are in America and Britain.

Russians like to drink. This applies especially to the men, but strong drink in regular quantities is beyond their economic means. Even so, the USSR has its share of alcoholics, I have known a few.

Now, in the above I have tried to say that with all their privation, the lack of a wide list of consumer goods, the restrictions on creative activities in the arts, a vast majority of Russians—to my conviction—would not pull up roots and given the chance settle in the West. Some would, and they have said so in front of me, but I think these would be relatively few in numbers.

In my husband's account of our first return to Russia in 1963, in his book *The Cossacks Burned Down the Y.M.C.A.*, he related how for ten long years I had talked to him of my desire to visit my homeland and how he finally took me back.

After we had spent six weeks in Moscow and made brief visits to other parts of the country—while our children remained in England—he recalled that one night, with the ruby lights of the electric stars above the Kremlin shining into our hotel rooms, I told him something that he had been waiting for years to hear.

"Honey," I said on that soft, spring, Muscovy night, "I want to go home."

How odd we mortals are. Here I am today, in late 1967, making plans to visit my mother in Mother Russia once more.

33 On that first return to Russia we brought back to England a number of trinkets and souvenirs which included what looked like two miniature Orders of Lenin, a very high decoration in the Soviet Union. I bought them at a Moscow street kiosk, and at the moment of purchase, I could not have guessed in a thousand tries to what eventual use they would be put.

One day the postman popped a large, square, thick envelope through our fortress-like front door. I opened this invitation—for that is what it was—and saw to my astonishment that Queen Elizabeth II and her husband Prince Philip had "Commanded" a secretary to invite us to a party at Windsor Castle. It was specific about dress—for men white tie, tails, and decorations.

"Decorations?" said my husband when I telephoned him at his office. "I don't have any decorations."

"Yes," said I, "that's something I've often wondered about. Other men have orders and decorations. Why don't you?"

"Because I was too young for the first war, and I reckon I was too old for the second."

"Too old?"

"Well, I really wasn't. I had to register for the armed forces and all that. This was back in the late nineteen thirties, before America got into the war. As you know, I was sent abroad as a foreign correspondent in nineteen forty."

"Yes, go on."

"Well, I was down in a miserable, flea-bitten hotel on

the Volga when I was awakened one night by a celebration staged outside my hotel door by the Japanese Naval Attaché and several of his friends. I didn't know it at the time, but they were celebrating Japan's attack on Pearl Harbor."

"Are you trying to tell me you volunteered?" I asked.

"Yes, I am. I sent a message from Kuibyshev on the Volga to the draft board in Washington offering my services as a soldier."

"I gather they didn't want you?"

"You're right. They told me to stay where I was; that I was of more service to my country as a war correspondent on the eastern front than I would be as an aging private on the western front. So"—and I could almost hear him shrug his shoulders—"that's the reason, and perhaps the only reason, why I have no decorations. I'm sure of two things though."

"What are they, Honey?"

"The first is, I seriously doubt if I could win a decoration."

"What's the second?"

"The second is, I'm tired of going to formal parties without decorations."

"What tires you about that?"

"Because, without a chest full of medals everyone takes me for a waiter, and they keep on asking me to get them drinks, or direct them to the men's room."

"But surely you're going to this party at Windsor Castle?"

"Oh, yes. And I'm going with decorations. Where are those miniature Orders of Lenin you bought in Moscow?"

"You wouldn't. You couldn't," I spluttered. "You wouldn't dare."

"If I can't wear them then I won't go."

Eventually—but not without a vigorous struggle—I gave in. And he wore them. I shall call no names, but during that evening at the castle a very handsome gentleman with a very handsome title stopped to say hello.

"What are those medals?" he asked.

The gentleman of title was standing too close to be bluffed or put off, so Eddy confessed all. This produced a loud laugh, so loud that the Queen, who was standing a few feet away, turned to stare.

"God of mine," I said to myself in Russian, "I beg of you don't let *her* look."

My prayer was answered, but the noble gentleman who was so amused at my husband's audacious wearing of two miniature Orders of Lenin—bearing the likeness of a man who helped topple an emperor—to a royal ball that he leaned forward and said, "Don't worry, old boy, they're just about as genuine as some of the medals being worn here tonight."

With that I took a close look at the pair of trinkets on my husband's left chest. Tinted in white and gilt enamel and hanging on neat little crimson ribbons, they did not look too bad. But, oh, suppose the Queen had asked about them? As it was once said about her great-great-grand-mother Queen Victoria, "Her Majesty was not amused." I seriously doubt that Queen Victoria's great-great-grand-daughter would have been amused either.

The ball at Windsor was given by the Queen and her husband for Princess Alexandra shortly before she married Angus Ogilvy, second son of the Earl of Airlie. Eddy and I had known Angus for years, but had the honor of being presented to Princess Alexandra only a few months before her engagement was announced. For a couple of reasons I shall always remember the evening of our meeting.

The occasion was a private, informal dinner at the Chelsea home of friends, and when we were invited the hostess did not mention that royalty would be present. As always, I am afraid I was late. In my defense I should say that living in Sussex nearly forty miles from London, it is not always easy to be on time when one has to drive up from the country. Anyhow, we were late and I was ashamed of myself. After being presented to Her Royal Highness, I apologized for our tardiness and she was most gracious in the way she accepted it.

A beautiful young woman, Princess Alexandra is kind, considerate, and a member of the royal family who makes you feel comfortable in her presence. She often represents the Queen at official functions and she does it extremely well, making friends for her country, her Queen, and herself.

At dinner that evening I was undergoing some gentle fun-making of my accent and the way I mix up words and phrases when speaking English too quickly. Looking across the candlelit table, Her Royal Highness joked with a sweet smile, "Tamara, if they bully you any more, come and sit here beside me. They won't dare bully you here."

On being presented to the Queen she is first addressed as "Your Majesty," and later simply as "Ma'am," which the British pronounce "Marm." With royal princesses, it is, of course, "Your Royal Highness" the first time and from then on, "Ma'am."

Sometimes the two are confused, especially by foreigners. At King Constantine's wedding, President Johnson's daughter addressed the King not as "Your Majesty," but as "Your Royal Highness." One would have thought that someone should have instructed her—and saw to it that she remembered. But Americans are an informal people and I am quite sure no one minded.

Being around royalty can be a tricky business.

Interviewing that nonconformist, kookeroo young actor David Warner recently, my husband was told an offbeat story of Warner's first experience of lunching at Buckingham Palace.

After his highly successful performance in *Morgan, A Suitable Case for Treatment*, the twenty-two-year-old actor, who, before his film debut, was a Shakespearian actor, was invited to the palace to lunch with the Queen and Prince Philip. Princess Marina, Duchess of Kent, a brigadier general, the president of an insurance company, and the metropolitan police commissioner were also guests.

"Once inside the palace," said Warner, "a charming man instructed me in protocol telling me I must wait for the Queen to speak to me first—before I spoke to her."

At lunch David was seated beside Princess Marina. She selected white wine. So he ordered white wine. After a few minutes the Queen turned to the actor and asked what parts he had been playing with the Royal Shakespeare Company.

"I told her 'Kings, Your Majesty,' and added that I was now playing Richard II—'the one they pushed off the throne.'

"For one awful moment I wondered if I had said the wrong thing. But everyone smiled and seemed to find my remark amusing, so I was able to relax a little."

When the dessert was served, Warner in his nervousness goofed it a bit by helping himself to a banana, an orange, an apple *and* a tangerine.

"Suddenly I looked around and realized that everyone else had finished, while I still had an apple to go," he told Eddy.

To his relief Princess Marina rescued him. She had one grape left on her plate. She had hung on to that single grape so that Warner would not feel too embarrassed by being the last to finish. She said to him, "If you eat your apple very quickly, I'll eat my grape very slowly—and then we'll finish together."

Continuing his account of the incident, Warner said to my husband, "So, she peeled her grape, split it in two, took out the stones and ate it very, very slowly, indeed. It was a charming gesture and it saved my face."

The daughter of Princess Marina, Princess Alexandra has that same thoughtfulness of others.

Earlier I said that there were two reasons why I shall always remember the evening of my meeting Princess Alexandra; the first being of course, the meeting itself.

The second is less pleasant.

After Her Royal Highness had left the party for her home in Kensington Palace, we said our farewells and started on our trip back to Sussex.

Just south of the River Thames a car piled into the side of our station wagon.

I suffered a mild concussion of the brain.

In a single evening I had experienced the pleasure of being presented to Princess Alexandra, and getting pranged in a car accident.

As Mr. Casey Stengel, the professor of baseball, philosophized in our house that evening he visited us:

"Life's a funny thing. You win a three straight in Boston and then drop a double-header in Washington."

34 To do a close up, intimate story of young King Constantine, my husband flew down to Athens, and on his first evening there had dinner at the big downtown palace with the King, his mother Queen Frederika, Queen Anne-Marie, and Princess Irene.

"What do you know about films?" asked the King, holding forth a pair of advertisements for movies. "After dinner we thought we could see one of these."

Noting that one starred Albert Finney, Eddy said he could assure his host of one thing—it would be well acted. On that advice the Finney film was selected.

After dinner and a great deal of good conversation, the royal family and my husband removed themselves to a long high-ceilinged room and in a deep comfortable chair Eddy was placed between Queen Frederika and Queen Anne-Marie, a seating arrangement that he felt was hardly likely to be repeated. As he put it, "A knave between queens, king high."

His earlier assurance that any role handled by Albert Finney would be more than completely acted was a correct one. But, the subject of the story was so unpleasant—a grisly murder with Finney keeping the head of his victim in a hat box—that his recommendation was far from a happy choice and as reel after reel of the murder graphically unrolled, Eddy felt more and more responsible for inflicting his host with a shocker. But if the King and his wife, mother and sister had been made uncomfortable by the movie they did not show it.

"Having such things happen to him," he said later, "comes under the divine right of kings, I suppose."

At last the film flickered to its macabre end and it was time to go.

"How do you call for a taxi from a king's palace?" Eddy asked himself, and then, after thinking it over, asked His Majesty, "May I use your telephone?"

"Of course," said King Constantine. "If you'll just come along here I'll show you where it is."

He led the way down a long spacious corridor and into a room still stacked high with wedding gifts.

"Are you sure you won't let me send you home in my car?" asked the King.

"Oh, no, sir. I'm going to join a late party with some friends. They told me they were practically your neighbors. If I can get them on the 'phone I won't need a taxi. They said they'd send for me."

"Before you call them," suggested the King of the Hellenes, "would you like to see some of our wedding presents? It's some job writing all the thank you letters, but we're getting it done. Here, let me show you a few. This one is from General and Mrs. de Gaulle."

At the telephone the King asked, "Do you know the number?"

"Yes, sir, I've got it here."

"Would you like me to dial it for you?"

"Oh, no, sir. I think I can manage it."

He managed.

"Ask them what entrance they'll be coming to?"

They told Eddy and he told the King.

After Eddy made his farewells, the King was so concerned that he might miss his friends that he accompanied my husband out of the front door, down the steps, into the driveway and actually out in the dark street. As a single automobile approached, the King said, "That should be your friends."

With profuse thanks for a delightful evening—with the exception of that film—Eddy said good night.

"I believe we are seeing you at my mother's for lunch tomorrow," said the King as they shook hands.

Lunch the following day was memorable for many reasons—Queen Frederika's hospitality, splendid food, and still another chance to talk at length and quite informally with this unusual family to whom the West and the opponents of Communism owe a great deal.

Although it was Saturday afternoon, the young King still had work to do, and said so.

"On Monday, Anne-Marie and I are going out to the country. I'm showing my country to her. I want her to know the people and the people to know her. I'd like you to come along. I think you'll find it interesting."

Repeating that he had work to do the King excused himself and went in search of his chauffeur. Queen Anne-Marie continued to carry on an animated conversation with her mother-in-law. While this was still in progress, King Constantine's handsome head appeared in the doorway and with a smile he said to his bride-wife:

"Hey, Queen, we've got to go!"

Later that year when the King and Queen came to London on business we had lunch with them at Claridge's, the four of us sitting at a table for four. The wine steward brought in that hostelry's long and impressive wine list and offered it to the King—who must be the world's most natural and unaffected monarch—for, turning to my husband, he asked, "Do you know anything about wine, because I don't."

The King ordered beer while Eddy ordered the wine.

Back at our house I asked, "What did it feel like when the King suggested you order the wine?"

"It was kind of nice," he replied, "but it made me homesick."

"Homesick? How could *that* make you homesick?"

"I seemed so far from the cotton fields of Alabama."

Later, after the state funeral of Sir Winston Churchill, we had another example of the King's unfailing thoughtfulness and his informal way of doing things.

As the world knows, the funeral was long, deeply moving and the day raw and cold.

While my husband sat at his typewriter at The Associated Press's London office—clicking out thousands of words about the historic event—I remained at Old Porch House with our then eight-year-old Natasha watching the funeral on television.

When everything was over Queen Elizabeth invited the kings, queens, heads of state, and other distinguished foreigners to Buckingham Palace for lunch. All morning long Natasha had seen so many kings, queens, princes, and princesses, that her little head was full of them. In that context I hope the following will be understood.

Well after the funeral, just as we heard my husband's car entering our driveway, the telephone rang and my daughter answered it. From an extension that I picked up I heard Natasha say, "East Grinstead 20."

"This is Buckingham Palace," began a deep voice on the other end of the line. "Is Mr. Gilmore there?"

"He's just come home," said our eight-year-old.

"Tell him the King would like to speak to him."

I love my daughter for many reasons, and I could have hugged her as I heard her child's voice ask:

"Which king, please?"

During those long terrible days when Sir Winston lay dying, and Eddy was writing thousands of words day and night about it, he received from the United States and elsewhere, many letters and telegrams. These messages were from people who had read his stories and they were unusually complimentary.

One night he said to me:

"A reporter's job is one at which he can never be completely successful, yet it's one to which he dedicates his life. In dedicating his life, he should always remember one thing—that it's life itself that is noble and grand, and not the guy reporting it. More important. He should always take his subjects seriously, but never himself."

"What are you getting at?" I asked.

"Well, when I began getting those telegrams about my Churchill stories I'm afraid I began taking myself pretty seriously, almost as seriously as my subject."

"What did you do?"

"I didn't do anything. Somebody else did it for me."

"Go on."

"Well, this morning, between the medical bulletins from No. 28 Hyde Park Gate (Sir Winston's London home), I was opening a fresh batch of telegrams and letters. I found one from an eleven-year-old girl from Moline, Illinois. It said:

"'Dear Mr. Gilmore:
I have been reading your wonderful stories about Sir Winston Churchill. Can you give me the home address of the Beatles?'"

I think Sir Winston Churchill was one of the greatest men in the world. So did my American husband. We greatly wanted something Churchillian; something that he had known and been around. Very luckily for us, Lady Spencer-Churchill, his widow, in disposing of much of the furniture from 28 Hyde Park Gate at a sale at Christie's, the fine arts auctioneers, offered a beautiful old mirror.

As the successful bidders, it now hangs in our drawing room.

35 Once upon a time an ancient Russian, with a beard that looked like it had been brooding birds for several seasons, told me that by nature the Slav is an emotional person given to transient periods of elation and gloom. He could be right. As a Slav I certainly have my ups and downs, but my ups are upper than my downs are down.

On one occasion—for no particular reason other than the sun was shining, the air warm, my husband and children well and happy and I was feeling fine—I decided to do something that I had wanted to do for a very long time. This was to take a bath in champagne.

I wonder how many people have had a similar urge? Some day I hope to poll my friends on the subject, for only then will I know that if in wanting to indulge myself in a champagne bath I may have been experiencing some sort of psychiatric disorder. I doubt this. I just wanted a champagne bath and I took one.

For those who have never tried it, let me emphasize that the actual physical contact with a load of champagne is not as glamorous as it may sound. The sensation is more subtle.

While having large supplies of champagne—the noblest of wines—seems to be a recurring problem in 1967, there have been moments when lashings of it happily seemed to be at hand. My champagne bath urge happily coincided with one of these. I had plenty of it, and a great deal of it was neither brut, sec, demi-sec, or doux, but blanc des blancs, of which not nearly enough is made.

Methodically, I more than half-filled my bathtub with this cool sparkling beverage, if such nectar can be classified as a beverage. I discovered that to half fill a bathtub with champagne takes more bottles than I imagined. As it was a hot day I did not have on many clothes and I removed these first and showered. Then, ever so delicately I stuck my right toe into the lovely liquid in my bath. I put both feet on the tub's bottom and eased myself beneath the surface. The sensation was delicious. I surfaced, lay back, and thoroughly enjoyed my bubbly soak. At last, I felt I had indulged myself enough. I got out as slowly as I had gotten in.

I suppose that very few things are absolutely, completely, unequivocally, unreservedly, fundamentally, emphatically, and clinically perfect. But my bath in blanc des blancs— with certain reservations—is the closest I have ever come to feeling that I was approaching the infinity of perfection.

Then the bubble burst.

Inside the skin champagne is heavenly stuff. Outside it is exceedingly sticky.

A second shower was imperative.

Still tingling, I faced up to a real challenge. However, I did manage to pull the plug on all that lovely drink.

That evening I joined Eddy for dinner at a new London night club. As we were dancing he asked:

"Do you smell vinegar?"

Now is not that an American husband for you?

As Casey Stengel rationalized on dropping a double-header to a tail-end team like Washington after racking up a consecutive streak of ball games in Boston, I too have my philosophy about life's law of averages.

With me, bad luck invariably follows a run of good.

Never since our marriage had we enjoyed such an unbroken stretch of good health as we were enjoying that

spring of my champagne ablution. We had even weathered
an English winter without so much as one cold. So, although the winds of spring were comfortable I felt it was
an ill wind blowing down the High Street.

I am unable to remember for what reason—my diary does
not show it—but Senator, now Vice President Hubert Humphrey, arrived in London on some mission, and agreed to
meet with a few members of the American press.

With others, Eddy was furiously writing away in his note-
book on whatever it was Mr. Humphrey was saying, when it
happened—a terrible pain stabbed my husband in the stomach. Trying not to show the agony he was going through,
he scribbled on, but minute by minute the pain worsened.
He stayed the course though, thanked Mr. Humphrey and
took a taxi to his office. Near fainting, he wrote his story,
hurried home and collapsed on the floor of the drawing
room.

Quickly summoned, our doctor ordered him to the hospital by ambulance and the offending gallstones and gall
bladder were removed.

I have never had the pleasure of meeting Vice President
Humphrey. I feel quite sure that he is a very nice man, but
after my husband's operation he received the following cablegram from the managing editor of a midwestern newspaper:

SORRY ABOUT THE GALL BLADDER. I HAVE KNOWN HUBERT
HUMPHREY LONGER AND MORE INTIMATELY THAN YOU. YOU
GOT OFF LIGHT.

My Old Man Volga had like Mr. Khrushchev the man
some say he resembles, a rubber ball's resilience to such mis-
adventures as illnesses, operations and hangovers, and was
soon back on the job to the obvious relief of myself and our
three daughters. As is usual with girls, ours adored their
father. They looked up to him, respected him and thought
he could do no wrong. I can recall but one incident when

they unanimously agreed that he had let them down. It was not long after he was separated from his gall bladder.

The occasion began at luncheon with Walter Shenson, the American-born producer of the Beatles' movies. After the meal Mr. Shenson suggested Eddy might be amused by watching the boys at work. On this particular day they were filming at a London theater rented by the film company for certain shots.

Backstage, away from the cameras, my husband met John, Paul, George, and Ringo, and as they talked, the producer said, "The scene we're working on this afternoon is supposed to be a press conference. Eddy, wouldn't you like to step in and play yourself?"

"Fine idea," said John Lennon.

Eddy thanked the Beatles and Walter Shenson, but refused. No amount of persuading budged him. When my daughters learned of this wholly out-of-character shyness from their extrovert parent they were deeply disappointed and, in shrill chorus, demanded an explanation.

"It was a question of hair," he explained. "You see, those guys have got so much and I've got so little, that the contrast would have been too shattering. My image couldn't stand it."

"Oh, Papa," said Natasha, "you don't know what you've done to me. If you'd acted with the Beatles I'd have been a hero for a whole week at school."

36 For one reason or another Sir Gerald Kelly spent ten years in doing my portrait. I hope that this does not mean that I am so ugly that it took a decade—my favorite new word a second time—to get my Slavic likeness on canvas in color.

Beginning the picture in 1956, Sir Gerald had to suspend operations when Natasha's birth drew near, for in my condition I found the sittings too exhausting. Following Natasha's appearance there was that year out of my active life because of tuberculosis. By the time I was up and about, the past President of the Royal Academy had been knocked down in a London street by an automobile. He recovered almost miraculously but then went down with dizzy spells. Just as he made a comeback from his latest misfortune I took off on a series of journeys, to America, South Africa and Moscow, but in the winter of 1965–66, he and I vowed the project must be finished. As Eddy was away on a lecture tour in the United States, this was not easy, for it meant that while the children were at school I had to travel up to London sit for Gerald and then board the train back to Sussex. I withstood this routine largely because of the splendid lunches furnished by the artist's darling wife, Jane, the Lady Kelly. The three of us ate in the kitchen, hard by Gerald's beloved wine cellar which must be one of England's most sumptuous long lines of cool bins in which nestle thousands of dusty bottles, containing vintage wines from some of France's most famous châteaux.

As I commenced my twice weekly journeys up to London

for the sittings, refreshing myself on Jane's delicious food and Gerald's wine, he took me by the hand on that first day of posing-eating-drinking, placed me in a strong light, examined my face as if he were looking for a bug on a lettuce, and said with his usual directness, "Well, my dear, you're not what you used to be, but we'll carry on as if nothing's happened."

I believe I would have toppled from my perch had not Lady Kelly, who was looking on, spoken to her husband very sharply saying, "Well, who is—are *you*?"

When we began I asked Sir Gerald if he could possibly finish the portrait by late February, 1966, for I was to meet my husband in Dayton, Ohio, toward the end of his lecture tour. Always the professional he applied the last stroke of the brush on schedule. I was much pleased with the result. While I had my reasons for getting the portrait completed in a hurry, the artist also had his. He told me that he planned to include the painting in the Royal Academy's summer exhibition.

England: what a country. Year after year its annual social season begins with the "Private View" of an art exhibition. This "Private View" is hardly as private as one might suppose, for in addition to one's self, another seven thousand or so guests are present. Yet, it is great fun.

People assemble in all sorts of clothes; in everything from gray-trousered, top-hatted morning attire to seaters and sockless sandaled feet.

I hope I may be forgiven for this, but I felt greatly thrilled at being hung in this great and ancient place, founded by King George III in 1768 with Sir Joshua Reynolds as its first president.

Pointing out that the summer exhibition included portraits of the Queen, the Queen Mother, and Prince Philip as well as Tamara Gilmore, a London newspaper commented that it could hardly imagine a more unusual transition than one

from a Siberian banishment by Joseph Stalin to the Royal
Academy by Sir Gerald Kelly.

In celebration of the portrait's completion and hanging,
Eddy on returning from his exhausting speaking tour of
forty-nine cities, took Lady Kelly, Sir Gerald, and me to
dinner at Claridge's. Few men can enliven a dinner party as
Gerald. At this one he proceeded to good-naturedly—but
with some feeling—lecture our waiter on the wrongness of
scooping cheese from the heart of a wheel of cheddar
weighing at least thirty pounds.

"You should never scoop cheese," said the artist staring
with disapproval over glasses resting on the tip of his nose.

"Excuse me, sir, but that's how we do it at Claridge's,"
came back the waiter.

"Then Claridge's bloody well does it wrong."

Royal Claridge's is not accustomed to such blunt criticism
from a Knight Commander of the Royal Victorian Order, or
from anyone else for that matter.

"I would like you to talk with the head waiter," said
the tail-coated servant at our table. "He will tell you, sir,
that I am serving this cheese correctly."

"Do as you wish about your head waiter," came back
Sir Gerald, "but when you serve it with a scoop you are
serving it incorrectly."

The head waiter appeared, as if from a trap door, and he
looked so much like what a head waiter should look like
that I wanted to laugh.

"And now, Sir Gerald," he began with what I thought
was a tone of lofty disdain, "what is all this about a scoop?"

In plain English Gerald told him.

"But, Sir Gerald, the custom was started by Queen Victoria when she presented the brigade of guards with a silver
scoop, and this scoop, if you will forgive me for saying so,
is an exact replica."

"Did you say 'Queen Victoria'?"

"Indeed I did, sir, for indeed it *was* Queen Victoria."

"Ah," said the past President of the Royal Academy, with reckless lese-majesty, "now I know I'm right.

"Now, see here, watch me closely and I shall show you how cheese should be properly served—with a knife—and for goodness sake, put away that ridiculous scoop."

Routed, the head waiter disappeared.

Among other distinguished men in England I feel honored to call a friend is the many-million-dollared American oil-man and art collector, J. Paul Getty. His home, Sutton Place, is near Guildford in County Surrey not far from us in Sussex, and shortly after he purchased it from the Duke of Sutherland, Mr. Getty invited us to see it firsthand, and filled with his treasures.

Patiently and carefully he conducted us through the stately rooms of this grand Elizabethan house, stopping to explain each painting, sculpture, tapestry, and piece of furniture. Then he took us outside to the kennels where live the fierce Alsatian dogs who, with their handlers, guard his grounds. Next he led us to the covered swimming pool he uses daily. As if saving the best for last he led us back inside Sutton Place to a butler's pantry and pointed with some pride to a pay station telephone he had only just installed.

"I'm getting tired of people coming down here and calling all over the world on my telephone," said Mr. Getty. "So I'm putting a stop to it. My friends won't mind paying for their calls and I don't care what the spongers think."

"But Paul," asked my husband of the man often referred to as the richest man in the world, "what are you going to do about the coins?"

"What coins?"

"Well, it's not everyone who has enough coins in his pocket to pay for a call to New York. Won't you defeat yourself when they ask you to lend them the coins? They're sure to say they have no change."

"I've thought of that," said J. Paul with a wry smile, "just walk over here with me."

Leading us to a cupboard he pulled out a drawer filled with all sorts of British coins; enough I would say to call Hong Kong.

"I still think you're defeating your purpose," said Eddy. "If you have to furnish the coins, it comes to the same thing as your having to pay for the calls."

"Not at all," said the oilman. "These coins are for making change when they plead they have nothing but one pound and five pound notes."

He touched his side pocket and smiled again as he said, "And I keep the key to the coin box!"

37 I do not like England. I love it, and so did Eddy, for many reasons.

It is, of course, a delightful land with ancient traditions, populated by a highly inventive and original people who, up until a few years ago, were ashamed, reluctant, or too shy to exploit their originality commercially.

They stage-manage pageantry better than anyone. Their long and opulent past has given them both opportunity and practice. In their new experience of being original, they tire too easily of their creations, and in fear of being faulted for hanging on, too long, abandon them.

Having surrendered its empire, old England is, in a way, like an elegant, still handsome, aged courtier who is living by his wits and experience, and of late, the daring innovations of precocious grandchildren. While the beautiful old gentleman has abandoned his once great riches overseas, his progeny at home has seized the lead in many facets of modern living.

London has become the world capital of male and female fashion. Its film producers, directors, actors and actresses make Hollywood seem old fashioned. The London theater sparkles with fresh ideas, and in presenting them to the public, wisely refrains from pricing themselves out of existence. Its young writers and performers, leaning heavily on television, revived satire, made it topical, biting and hilarious, but having done this they now seem timid about keeping it up, or developing it further. Perhaps it is another case of becoming bored too quickly.

By freezing wages in the midst of prosperity, Britain's Labor Government seems to me to have performed a remarkable and courageous act. How many workers' governments have been daring enough to order their trade unions to cease their shrill claims for higher wages and shorter work weeks? I can understand this sort of thing being done by conservative governments (although I cannot understand why Britain's last one did *not* do so), but in my political naïveté I do admire a Labor Government for so acting.

On the less serious side, Britain's customs are delightfully bewildering.

Officers of the elite Coldstream Guards do not toast the Queen, taking the position that as they restored the Monarchy they hardly have to toast a Sovereign who, to their way of thinking, owes his or her throne to them.

In the British Army sergeant-majors are not addressed as sergeant major, or even sergeant or sarge, but as "Sar," not "Sir," please—just "Sar."

There is another military unit whose officers keep their caps on when making the loyal toast. Aboard ship the Royal Navy does its toasting seated.

To the discomfort of many visiting Americans, tobacco is not smoked at formal luncheons and dinners before the loyal toast.

Port, for some reason, is always passed around the table clockwise.

Where else but in England can you find the owner of a large and beautiful country house greeting a guest who arrived for the weekend accompanied by three servants, with the declaration, "I'm terribly sorry your gardener is ill."

"Ill?" asked the surprised and new-rich guest. "My gardener's not ill. What makes you think he is?"

"Because," replied the host, shifting his pale blue eyes to the trio of servants, "if he were not ill, I'm sure you would have brought him too."

Is there any other place but England where one could

have encountered a seventy-two-year-old, but well-preserved actor, arriving at another weekend house party with a seventeen-year-old girl, and accused by his host of carrying things too far, explained, "But Charles, I'm afraid you don't understand. At my age and station in life I am getting a certain satisfaction in hissing my own performance."

Then there is the young man in the British Foreign Office who was assigned to accompany an American senator visiting London.

Mr. John Hay Whitney was the United States Ambassador at the time. When he moved into Winfield House he brought with him many of the paintings from his remarkable collection. As the young Englishman arrived with the senator in tow—his eyes swung immediately to the majestic oils on the walls about him. I am not sure what the American lawmaker was looking at—if anything—for he seemed surprised when the Foreign Office junior said to Mr. Whitney, "I must say, Mr. Ambassador, how much I am enjoying your pictures."

Looking up, the senator is reported to have said, "Pictures? Whitney, I didn't even know you painted."

The British have mastered the art of the perfect squelch in the form of a question.

One night at London's Planetarium, Mr. Salvador Dali, the surrealist painter—and surrealist talker—was making a speech which was a mixture of double-talk, swallowed words, and involved phrases. When he finished a man in the audience—a very young man—stood up and asked Mr. Dali:

"Sir, I have been sitting here for the last thirty minutes listening to you very carefully, and I haven't understood a single thing you've said. Tell me, should I be ashamed or should you?"

And the names of places and people. How they delight. Cholmondeley is pronounced "Chumly." Featherstonehaugh is "Faneshaw." Cockburn—"Coburn." Belvoir—"Beaver."

To taste bubble-and-squeak and toad-in-the-hole may be

no epicurean's pleasure, but in a restaurant I find sheer joy in just letting the words roll off my tongue.

In these streamlined times of mini-skirts, mini-cars and mini-steaks, what a delightful surprise it is to find a gentleman whose full name and title is:

Admiral the Honorable Sir Reginald Aylmer Ranfurly Plunkett-Ernle-Erle-Drax.

Living in England, with the happy opportunity of returning often to the United States and Russia to see relatives and friends and to recharge our spiritual and emotional cells, I think that my American husband and I enjoyed the best of three worlds.

38 If America and Russia are unable to exist without conflict of interests and ideologies, bickering and hints at war, how is it that an American and a Russian were able to live happily together for a quarter of a century?

My husband and I were so different that I was constantly amazed we got along at all.

He liked jazz. My preference is for classical and semiclassical music. He salted his food. I do not. I am always late. He was punctual. He was unable or unwilling to bargain over anything, while I believe I could hold my own in an Arab bazaar in the frenzy of Shawwal, those first frantic days following Ramadan. He preferred modern furniture. I go for Messrs. Chippendale, Sheraton, and Hepplewhite. I adore jewelry to which he was indifferent. He liked hot cakes and syrup which I abhor. He wanted my hair long. I am sure it looks best short. Eggs repel me. They were his favorite food. With difficulty I can recognize a Rolls-Royce, but I would have trouble in trying to name any other car on the world market; but Eddy could identify them all from a quarter mile distance. Fish is my dish. Ham was his. He rose with the sun. I can lie in bed all day. I go for long skirts. He preferred minis. I am afraid of cows. He could even milk them. Claret was his favorite wine. Champagne is mine. He would go into a state of ecstasy over hot biscuits and butter. I prefer cold black bread. In patent leather shoes I enjoy a feeling of well being. He shunned them, saying they not only looked cheap, but reflected my panties. In the theater I am carried away by ballet. Eddy Gilmore would have rather watched acrobats and plays by Chekhov. For me walking is a relaxation; for him it was hard on the feet and a chore. At a baseball game he was in seventh heaven. I have yet to discover what goes on. He liked riding on trains. That is my idea of nothing to do. A shower was his mode of bathing, the tub mine. As for reading matter, he was entranced by the Russian novelists Dostoyevsky, Turgenev, and Tolstoy. I am happiest with romances, the more romantic the better. Among poets I champion Alexander Pushkin and Mikhail Yurevich Lermontov. He said they were all right, but claimed that Robert W. Service, Kipling, and Robert Frost were more to his liking. I am terrified of the dark. My husband would walk into the darkest forest on the blackest of nights. In his whole life he never smoked as many as a dozen cigarettes while I am an addict. A full moon mesmerized him. It leaves me as cold as its pale light. He never once raised a hand to our children. A strong believer in corporal punishment, I would not go as far as George Bernard Shaw, who is reported to have said, "Never strike a child except in anger, otherwise he won't know why you are beating him," but I slap and spank my daughters when they are naughty. My husband scoffed at the suggestion that ghosts exist. I not only believe in them, I have seen them. I prefer soft beds. He liked them hard. He doted on fried oysters. I had just as soon eat fried snakes. He had a liking for the works of Vincent Van Gogh and Paul Gauguin, two painters I cannot abide. He called corn-on-the-cob a delicacy. I think it is hog food. He seldom gambled. I will bet on anything. He liked me to wear one-piece bathing suits rather than Bikinis, while I—under the correct conditions—prefer swimming nude.

How did two persons of such enormously dissimilar tastes, beliefs, backgrounds, likes, dislikes, fetishes, customs and characteristics manage to live together, much less remain happy?

I would be lacking in frankness if I did not confess that during our ten years together in Russia my husband and I had our share of domestic crises. While living in the United States we staggered through one big one, *but*—during our thirteen years in England—a country foreign to both of us— life was as blissful as an Hawaiian honeymoon.

Now if an American and a Russian—and a Soviet Russian at that—could get along so splendidly, why cannot their two Governments?

Mr. David Ben-Gurion of Israel once developed a charming theory of how a small nation, fighting for survival in a world of massive cartels and power politics, can enrich its economy beyond all belief. He said the tiny country should declare war on the United States in the most aggressive manner and, of course, suffer the inevitable ignominious defeat. This having been achieved in the absolute, Mr. Ben-Gurion claimed—and I am sure he is right—America would then rush to the aid of its prostrate victim and shower it with billions of dollars in foreign aid, thereby guaranteeing the Tom Thumb nation's economy for generations to come.

If Mr. Ben-Gurion can put forward a theory on the salvation of one minute country, I who have been a citizen of the two most powerful nations in the world, may surely be forgiven for suggesting mine.

The Tamara Gilmore theory is:

When the Americans and the Russians reach the moon —as they most assuredly will and soon—all will be well.

Free of their environment and liberated from their festering nationalism, they will dwell on the moon in sublime harmony, sending back masterful directives to their earthbound worshipful Governments that all Russians and Americans should forget their differences and unite in one monumental nose-thumbing at Mao Tse-tung and his bumptious Chinese.

DATE DUE